CHOICE PARENTING

Raise a caring, responsible child with

CHOICE PARENTING

*A more connecting, less controlling way
to manage any child behavior problem*

Richard Primason, Ph.D.

iUniverse, Inc.
New York Lincoln Shanghai

CHOICE PARENTING
A more connecting,
less controlling way to manage any child behavior problem

iUniverse, Inc.

For information address:
iUniverse, Inc.
2021 Pine Lake Road, Suite 100
Lincoln, NE 68512
www.iuniverse.com

ISBN: 0-595-32025-2

Printed in the United States of America

For Abbe, the best choice I ever made.
And for Philip and Ethan,
who make me proud every day.

ACKNOWLEDGEMENTS

The collection of counselors, teachers, and students who make up the choice theory community has been so important to the writing of this book. Their generosity and support have inspired my activity, inside and outside of the office. Of course Dr. Glasser deserves the credit for creating this community, and suggesting in such a respectful and powerful way that we live by the principles of choice theory. I'd like to thank John Brickell, Nancy Buck, William Glasser, Al Katz, and Robert Wubbolding for reading the early drafts, and helping me to shape my ideas into a book of some quality.

CONTENTS

PREFACE

Have you ever been stuck in a Chinese finger puzzle? You know, the woven paper tube that you slip your index fingers into, and then try to get out of? It's a paradox. The harder you pull, the more difficult it is to get free. To get the result you want, you have to do something very different than what you are inclined to do.

This book focuses on a similar paradox. It is called choice psychology, an approach that gives you more when you control less. It's not easy to resist the impulse to control your child; it's often the thing you're most inclined to do. But when you use the ideas described here, you'll actually end up with more of what you want as a parent. Choice psychology is a better answer for child behavior problems because it leads to the outcome you want most—a more caring, more responsible child.

Most people seeking guidance for parenting problems want techniques. *Tell me what I should say…Tell me what I should do,* are common requests, but without a guiding philosophy, techniques soon become ineffective. In my clinical practice, I explain to parents who are struggling with their children that they need a better way to think about behavior problems, an approach that is quite different from the conventional "reward and punish" psychology of our time. I offer them what is presented here, a psychology of choice.

This approach is based largely on *choice theory* (1998), a model of human behavior developed by renowned psychiatrist William Glasser. I had been reading his work for years, but it wasn't until I trained with his institute and had a chance to exchange ideas with Dr. Glasser that I began to fully understand his unique philosophy. As I learned, I not only became a more effective psychologist, I also became a better husband and father.

Choice theory suggests a rigorous ownership of responsibility for behavior, and allows no external excuse for emotional experience. Unhappiness is not something that happens to us, it's the result of choices we've made. Sometimes they're the best choices available, and sometimes they're the only ones we know how to make, but we are always capable of learning to do better. We are then responsible for our anger, our anxiety, and our depression. As explained throughout this book, we have chosen these emotional responses.

This new psychology of choice is offered in contrast to the more prevalent *external control psychology*. With that perspective, people blame their distress on forces outside of themselves and don't feel responsible for their own happiness. One example is the disturbing trend to view so many child difficulties as diagnosable psychiatric syndromes and to rely heavily on medication and other control strategies to address them. Schools, too, are often bastions of external control thinking, emphasizing compliance and conformity rather than fun and learning. The sad result is too many children who cope poorly at school and play, and feel ill equipped to create their own solutions to life's problems. The most thorough presentation of these contrasting *internal and external control models* is contained in <u>Choice Theory</u> (1998), Dr. Glasser's very readable summary of his ideas.

As I gained a deeper understanding of choice theory, my work with children and families began to change. Parents with highly defiant children continued to ask for better methods of control, but I began to offer them an alternative. I taught them to shift their whole approach from controlling to connecting, and they found their children to be more cooperative. I asked them to view their children's disruptive behavior as legitimate attempts to meet emotional needs, and they began to make better agreements together. At home, my own household became more peaceful. There were fewer ultimatums and confrontations, and more plans and choices. At times the application of this new way of thinking was very awkward; it was especially tough to give up my reliance on anger and punishment. But, it's hard to argue with success, and I was having a lot more of it.

The first section of this book is conceptual. It lays out the important elements of choice psychology[1], or internal control thinking. There is strong scientific support for this cognitive-behavioral model of human psychology, and much of it can be found in an excellent book called <u>Reality Therapy for the 21st Century</u> <u>(2000)</u>. In it, Dr. Robert Wubbolding summarizes the empirical research for the principles of choice theory and for its application to many areas including addiction, depression, education, and children's self concept.

The second section is called "A Better Set of Tools." It contains the new techniques that I teach to parents and children as they shift from control to choice

---

[1] The term *choice psychology* is my own name for a mind-set that is informed by Glasser's *choice theory*, and it is generally synonymous with his term *internal control psychology*.

parenting. It also covers the limitations of the old tools: *reinforcement, punishment*, and *time out*. There are suggested interventions and examples of a new way of speaking with your child about issues and problems. I try to make clear, however, that there's no magic in these suggestions. Choice parenting isn't really about saying the right words; it's about the intention behind them. Choose the techniques that make sense to you, or better yet, develop your own. As you continue to use this model, your responses will become clearer and more natural.

In the third section I discuss specific behavior problems that I encounter most frequently in my office practice. Very little emphasis is placed on diagnostic labels and clinical disorders. While such descriptive categories have their uses, I'm far more impressed with their overuse and harmfulness. A child with a disorder label such as "ADD" or "Bipolar" can easily come to think of himself as damaged or disabled. As a choice parent, you'll convey confidence in your child's capabilities and discourage excessive accommodation due to special diagnostic conditions.

This is not a book about child development, but I have tried to use examples of choice parenting with children of varying ages. This should help you see how principles of choice psychology can be applied throughout the stages of your child's life. You can find a thorough developmental model based on choice theory in Nancy Buck's very informative book, Peaceful Parenting (2000).

I should also mention that I generally use the masculine gender when writing about children in this volume. This choice was made purely for editorial convenience; it isn't meant to imply anything about the relative behavior of boys and girls. I hope that this convention won't be too much of a distraction to you.

With choice psychology, you can become a more effective, connected, and satisfied parent. As you do, you will raise children who are competent and satisfied. When they challenge you with difficult or upsetting behavior, you'll respond with a better understanding of their needs, and with a new range of choices. The book contains many examples of how to talk with your children and how to help them solve problems. Use these examples as a guide, and develop your own plan to change the psychology in your home. Throughout the text you'll find boxes labeled *"Think it Over, Write it Down,"* and other sections that ask for examples from your own experience. You might want to have a pencil handy as you read. The more involved with this material that you choose to be, the more helpful you'll find it.

SECTION ONE
A PSYCHOLOGY OF CHOICE

1. THE BEST OF INTENTIONS

Most parents have the best of intentions when it comes to raising their children. They want them to be safe, happy, and productive. It doesn't always work out so well; sometimes one or more of their children develop behavioral or emotional problems. Typically, parents consult me when their children are disruptive, with tantrums and defiance, or under-functioning due to anxiety or depression. Others seek guidance about a better way to help their "ADD" children who are struggling at school or with friendships. In all cases, the parents are concerned and frustrated, as the conventional methods that they've tried are not helping all that much. They've learned about effective communication and naturally occurring consequences. They've tried their best to use charting, contracting, and consistent limit setting. They may even have given their children psychoactive medications in order to control their symptoms. Although these parents get some relief, the children usually revert to behavior that is seriously upsetting to the family. Why aren't they getting more effective results—more long-lasting change?

Most of the conventional guidance that parents receive is fundamentally misguided. It's well intended, but simply off the mark. The conventional guidance in behavior management leads parents to work harder at controlling their children's behavior but only compounds the underlying problems of misunderstanding, frustration, and unhappiness. What these parents really need is a completely different way to think about parenting their children. They need an approach that strengthens family relationships and results in happier and more competent children. They need to consider a better choice.

Protecting and Preparing

As parents, we do our best to protect our kids from danger and to prepare them for a world of challenge and opportunity. Of course people vary in parenting style, and particularly in the degree to which they emphasize the protect or prepare functions (Baumrind, 1991). Protectors are nurturing and tend to be more indulgent parents. Preparers are concerned about limits and standards and tend to be more authoritarian. Most of the parent-to-parent conflicts that I see involve this prepare/protect debate. In reality, one style is no better or worse than the other. Each one has the potential to encourage children's internal development, or to stifle it. It depends on the philosophy of control that underlies the parenting style.

> *Whether a "protector" or a "preparer", every parent should guard against using external control psychology.*

Despite the best intentions, and plenty of well-meaning advice, we're raising too many children who are ill equipped to face their world without behavior problems, emotional distress, and personal disconnection. Parents have never been so educated and informed, and yet children exhibit the same degree of clinical problems that they always have, and some research suggests that they may actually be doing a bit worse (U.S. Public Health Service, 2001).

The problem is external control—the pressure we bring to bear on our children to become the people we desperately want them to be. Whether our preferred parenting style is one that emphasizes clear limits or one more focused on a child's needs and feelings, each one is susceptible to the same critical error of relying heavily on a psychology of external control. We use rewards to pressure our children to behave "appropriately," and we use punishments to "teach them a lesson" when their choices are poor ones. We jump too quickly to solve their problems, protecting them from stressors that are "making them upset." Teachers and friends tell us to "control our children," and this all makes sense to us because we live in a culture that is heavily reliant on external control. We're accustomed to a *control psychology*—a belief system that says that it makes sense to put pressure on people to make them behave the way we think they should. And what's so wrong with that? Shouldn't we do everything in our power to make sure that our children grow up properly?

The main problem with control psychology is that it really doesn't work very well. Talk to anyone who has a child with seriously challenging behavior, such as aggression or passive defiance, and you'll find a parent who has tried all of the usual control methods. They've used the charts and the points, and they've resorted to more heavy-handed control such as screaming, threatening and even some hitting. Their efforts may have shut down the behavior for a short time, but when they took a step back, the problem recurred. For many, it's a repeating cycle of frustration and discouragement. One parent told me, *"…external control requires constant vigilance. I just get tired of doing it after a while!"* I meet parents like this every day. They have the best of intentions but continue to use the ineffective, control-based methods they've been encouraged to employ. When I suggest they try a completely different approach, they tell me that yes, they'd very much like to. When we begin to talk about *choice psychology*, they often ask why no one has ever suggested this to them before.

> ## CONTROL PARENTING BELIEFS
>
> *I can make my child behave properly.*
>
> *Rewards and incentives are good ways to get children to meet their responsibilities.*
>
> *My child is too upset to meet his responsibilities.*
>
> *Children should pay a price for their bad behavior.*
>
> *My child's behavior can make me miserable.*

To parent by choice means to employ an entirely different psychology than the one that we're all accustomed to. While control psychology says that we can use pressure to get people to do what we want, choice psychology says that *everyone always chooses his or her own behavior.* Of course there's much more to it, but this simple idea is really the essence. It may seem trivial, and yet when you roll out the parenting implications of this simple shift in thinking, the difference in the way that you relate to your children and respond to their challenging behavior is quite profound.

> # *CHOICE PARENTING BELIEFS*
>
> *Children choose their own behavior.*
>
> *External pressure always exacts a cost.*
>
> *Children want to learn from their mistakes.*
>
> *We're all responsible for our own happiness.*

Sculpting and Gardening

I have a friend who is a sculptor, and he works in all different media. He is always shaping objects. He has an idea in his mind of how he wants the piece to look, and he works it and works it, trying to get as close as he can to the picture in his mind. Some people parent this way. They are sculptors, trying with the best of intentions to shape their children into a picture that they have in their mind. This is the essence of control psychology—that if you keep working it, you can get the world to look the way you want it to.

My wife is a wonderful gardener. She also has a picture in her mind, but she knows that there are elements of gardening that are largely out of her control. She can choose a location and cultivate the soil. She can select seeds or plantings and nurture them lovingly. But she must accept this simple truth: The plants she cares for have their own life force that will be expressed. She can choose her own gardening behavior. With reasonable care her plants will flourish, but no manner of intensive effort will change a shrub rose into a climber. Of course she can damage her plants through over-involvement or neglect, but she can never make them better than they are inclined to become by way of their own intrinsic energies and impulses. A good gardener understands that she chooses her behavior, and her plants choose their own.

> *Marianne did poorly in school when she was a child, and she is determined that her daughter will not repeat her mistakes. She has strict guidelines about when 9-year-old Suzie must do her homework. Sometimes Suzie, an*

excellent student, wants to play with a friend after school and asks if "just for today" she can do her work later. Marianne is kind but firm in her reply.

> *"No Honey, you'll just have to trust me on this—I know what's best for you."*

Marianne is trying to sculpt her daughter's life.

P.J. had been having some minor trouble over the past week with a "mean kid" in his second-grade class. Today he told his Dad that the boy drew an ugly picture of him and really hurt his feelings. Robert, P.J.'s Dad, was quite upset, and his first impulse was to call the school. First, he asked his son,

> *"What do you think you want to do about this?"*

P.J. said that he'd had about enough and was thinking of telling the teacher.

> *"Does that make me a snitch?" he asked.*

His Dad replied,

> *"You don't usually tell on people—no, I don't think you're a snitch. Sometimes telling the boss is the best choice, though. I guess you'll just have to figure out what feels right to you in this case."*

Robert is quite a good gardener.

I talk to dozens of parents each week about their struggles with child behavior problems. It becomes clear to me very early in the conversation if I'm dealing with a sculptor or a gardener. Some just naturally understand that their children are determined to become who they will become and that there's very little they can do to shape them into someone different. Of course we need to guide our children and teach them the choices that we believe are best. But we also have the capacity to use our power to control their choices. If this is our fundamental orientation to the job—if we are essentially external control parents, then we may do our children considerable harm and disrupt their own job of becoming the best person that they are determined to become.

THINK IT OVER, WRITE IT DOWN...

When have you parented more like a sculptor than a gardener?

_____

_____

_____ .

Parents who use choice psychology are by no means hands-off parents. They love their children and recognize their responsibility to assist in their children's development. Like a caring and careful gardener, choice parents select materials and make important choices in their own behavior. They create the proper conditions for successful growth, but go easy on control. Choice parents are unquestionably involved with their children, offering guidance and listening with interest to the children's view on whatever the latest social or practical challenges may be. The choice parent is in no way an indulgent parent. She recognizes that she must limit her own assistance and allow her children to develop their own plans and solutions.

Children of parents who use choice psychology deeply appreciate this special kind of involvement; they incorporate the parts of their parents' guidance that are consistent with their own picture of who they want to become. Choice parents are careful not to control their children's behavior because they recognize that it is essentially futile to do so. They understand that one can certainly try to control, or engage in what I call _control maneuvers,_ but that this will, over time, lead to a disconnection and less parental influence.

THINK IT OVER, WRITE IT DOWN...

When have you done some of your best parent gardening?

_____

_____

_____ .

I expect that a lot of questions are occurring to you. You may be wondering if choice parenting is a lenient approach that lets children "get away with" negative behavior. You may be thinking, "sure, maybe for someone else, but you haven't met my child." Or perhaps you're thinking, "Yes, I like the sound of that. But how do you actually <u>do</u> it?" These are the questions I often hear as I introduce choice parenting to frustrated moms and dads. All these questions will be thoroughly discussed in the pages that follow. In my clinical practice I routinely see children and parents who present with the most challenging behavioral and emotional problems. While not all of them adopt the choice psychology viewpoint, most do. And virtually all of those who become choice parents report distinct improvements in the relationships with their children. Remember, these are the most difficult cases I'm talking about, people who have been practicing external control for years. For the vast majority of you, a good-faith effort to consider this new way of parenting will yield clear and lasting benefits—for you and your child.

2. THE CORD THAT CONNECTS YOU WITH YOUR CHILD

Imagine a cord between you and your child. I think of it as a string of fine silk, but it can be anything that represents the connection between you. You know that when this cord is sound, it feels good to be with your son or daughter. At other times, especially if you've been struggling to control your child's difficult behavior, you don't feel well connected at all. That's because we all have a built-in need for freedom, and when your children sense that someone is trying to control them, they attend to their freedom need by disconnecting, at least a little bit. The irony is that when your children are having trouble sorting out difficult choices, they need their connection to you most of all. I suggest that this cord of connection become the central concept in your new way of thinking about parenting. Your paramount concern is to protect this cord.

I like the image of a cord to represent the relationship between parent and child—it conveys an open channel for communication, and for nurturance, guidance and support. Now we've all heard the advice, "Hey, it's time to cut the cord," which of course means that at some point you shouldn't be so closely involved in your children's lives as when they were younger. So when is the right time to cut it? In my vision, that connection between you might change over time, but it should continue to be a strong source of encouragement and shared experience through adolescence and beyond. I don't buy the conventional idea that teenagers aren't interested in their parents' points of view. The more difficult the choices that they face, the more they need your counsel. You see, while you may not have much direct control over your child's behavior, the influence that you do have is related to the quality of your relationship.

When I'm working with a father who feels trapped in a frustrating control struggle with his son, I ask if he thinks his child knows what is expected of him. The parent invariably replies, "Yes, of course he knows—he just refuses to do it."

Alex is such a parent, a well-intentioned father of a spirited 15 year old, Peter, who is ignoring the family's curfew rules. He isn't always home late, but often enough, and sometimes the lapses are real doozies! Each time Peter comes in later than the established curfew, Alex "goes ballistic." Their relationship is deteriorating, and Alex's wife is worried that her husband is pushing Peter further away. Of course their troubles didn't start here; their contest of control vs. freedom has a long history. Regardless of the past, this is where they are today. So I ask Alex if his son knows what the curfew is, and Alex reports that he's quite sure that he does. I suggest that he no longer needs to remind him, either before Peter goes out or after he arrives home. He already knows what's expected, and the repeated lectures seem to be ineffective, so I suggest that Alex relieve himself of this responsibility and instead focus on the connection between them. "Do you think you can do this, Alex?" I ask with concern. "Are you willing to try something very different that might help things to improve?"

Alex is a bit thrown off by my suggestion. He agreed to come in with his wife for this consultation, and he knows that their past efforts to control Peter have not worked out. He asks, "I'm not supposed to say anything at all when he comes in at 2:00 a.m.?"

I tell him that eventually he can ask Peter how he thought he handled last night's curfew, but that I'm not sure he's ready for this step. It should only be asked with curiosity, and not with any anger or accusation. I further explain to Alex that his son will be more concerned with honoring his agreements with his father when he feels well connected with him. I invite Alex to stop trying to control Peter's curfew behavior and focus instead on repairing a cord between them that is thankfully not broken, but certainly a bit worn. With his wife's encouragement and promise of support, Alex reluctantly agrees.

Okay, I know what many of you are thinking. "Let him get away with coming in at 2:00 a.m.? That's crazy!" I know, but just hear me out. You see, if Alex or his wife thought that there was a real safety issue at stake here, then I wouldn't have suggested this as a starting place. But they didn't, and nothing they were doing was helping, and the relationship between Alex and his son was going south in a hurry. This teenager was fast approaching a time where many safety issues would be in play. This is what was really scaring Alex and fueling his frustration and anger every time his son came home late. The idea of strengthening the cord and thereby improving the chances that Peter would value his father's guidance in the future made a lot of sense to Alex, and so his new work at becoming a choice parent began.

Strengthening the cord is a mutual affair, neither one of you can impose a good relationship. You try your best though, because you care deeply. You actually have a "built-in" need to have caring relationships, a need we'll talk more about in Chapter 4. Happily, your child has the same interest, and probably wants to feel well connected with you.

With Alex and Peter, the destructive control maneuvers had been going on for quite a while. Peter's built-in interest in being connected with his dad was not readily apparent—but it was still there. With support and encouragement from his wife, Alex was able to stop battling with his son about curfew, and other things as well. He invited Peter to spend time with him and do things that they used to enjoy together. It took a while before Peter agreed, but soon they had a Sunday morning routine that included going out for breakfast. It wasn't easy for Alex to refrain from criticizing Peter during their breakfast conversations, but that is exactly what his homework was. He kept at it, because he couldn't deny the results. The less he tried to control, the more connected he felt, and the more connected to the family Peter began to act. For Alex, the key to strengthening the cord was to stop correcting and instead ask Peter how he thought he was handling the various choices that came his way. That's called "self evaluation," one of 5 new tools described in Section Two.

The built-in need that you and your child have for connecting with others gives you a head start in repairing strained relations. I'll talk later about many different ways to strengthen the cord by approaching parent-child problems with choice psychology, and I'll also describe the typical ways that people weaken that cord despite their good intentions.

THINK IT OVER, WRITE IT DOWN...

When do you feel especially well connected with your child?

_____

_____

_____.

Some children come into this world with less natural ability to connect. It doesn't mean that they don't have the interest, but they are lacking an intuitive sense of how to read social nuance, and how to generally "fit in" with the social group. Some of these kids are given labels such as *learning disabled, attention deficit disordered, asperger syndrome, or developmental disordered.* Their parents have a special challenge, because regardless of a child's innate strengths and liabilities, his or her success in life depends on effectively connecting with others. Not everyone can be a social star, but in order to be happy you must have some satisfying relationships. Parents of these special children need choice psychology even more than most, and they should take heart. Even the most "disabled" children can have success finding their way in the social world. I'll talk about some general strategies for parenting special needs children in a later section.

My message is really quite simple. This cord between you and your child should be your paramount concern. Whenever you can, and especially when times are tough, do what you can to strengthen the cord. Try to stay connected—work hard to protect that relationship. When is the right time to cut the cord? I would say…never.

3. CONTROL PSYCHOLOGY: The Way of the World

The Control Imperative

We're all control freaks, and that's not really such a bad thing. After all, we really do want to be in control of our lives. We want a sense of assurance that if we choose action "a" then outcome "b" is likely to follow. That's why I have a favorite restaurant—I believe that I'm likely to have a great meal when I go there. Sometimes it works out that way, and I'm happy. Some people are so intent upon having things their way, they push and pressure and manipulate people to make it so. They are following a *control psychology* that says...

> *...it makes sense to use power to compel people to do things your way.*

Unfortunately, this is the prevailing psychology of the world. People who have power tend to use it to maintain the order that supports their power. But there's a big difference between seeking control in your own life and controlling the lives of others. Having a sense of *inner control* means that you know what you want and need, and you have a reasonable idea of how to get it. When the world cooperates and your plan works, you may get quite a bit of what you want. That's a good day. That match between what you want and what you actually get is as good a definition of happiness as I can think of.

That's what we're all trying to get control of—a reliable way to balance the two worlds that we live in. There's our *inner world,* the collection of ideas and pictures of the way we'd like things to be, and then of course there's the *outer world,* the collection of real-life events and behavior generated by other people. All we can do is choose behavior, and we're always making choices with the intent of bringing these two worlds into balance. We choose a neighborhood to live in that matches our *inner world* picture of how we'd like to live; we choose social activities that match our *inner world* picture of how we'd like to spend our time. When our choices are effective, we have a very satisfying inner control feeling.

Balancing Our Worlds

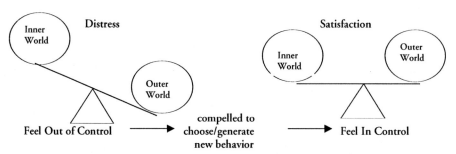

When our worlds are out of balance, we experience a distress that we are compelled to try to remedy. We must find some way to restore balance, and this is the *control imperative*. We will always generate some response—make some attempt to change the world in order to bring it into better alignment with our world. If I arrive at my favorite restaurant only to discover the chef has quit, then my worlds are out of synch, and I have an uneasy feeling in my gut. I immediately begin to generate behavior. I might pout and complain, question the management, or head out for my second-favorite restaurant. What you can be sure of is that I will do something, because the control imperative demands that I generate behavior aimed at restoring balance between my two worlds, restoring that sense of inner control. The control imperative doesn't demand that I impose my will on other people, but it does point me in that direction. It takes a real effort to resist following a control psychology.

Some people's responses to imbalance are quite visible. They might shout or stamp their feet. Sound like anyone you know? Others are quite private with their behavior, but don't be fooled into thinking they're not responding. They might silently wring their hands or secretly decide to do this or that, or maybe they tense up and generate a headache or a muscle spasm. These efforts may or may not be effective, but they all represent attempts to restore a sense of inner balance and control. So why does the word "control" have such a negative connotation?

Again, it's all about the difference between the pursuit of inner control, and the attempt to control others. When we try to determine the behavior and choices of others, they don't like it. It inhibits their basic need for freedom. Therein lies the major cause of conflict in parenting and all other relationships. **When someone in our world is not providing satisfying behavior, the control imperative suggests that we try hard to change them. They don't like it, and they tend to push back.**

When your daughter is watching "too much" TV, what does that really mean? It means that her behavior doesn't match your inner world picture, and you might tell her to turn it off. When your son is crying with hurt feelings, his mood doesn't match your inner picture of how you want him to feel, and so you do your best to comfort him. When your teenager's vulgar language offends you, you probably feel like telling him to shut up!

Remember the cord? Well, if it's strong and healthy, it's got a good deal of forgiveness in it. A sound relationship will tolerate a reasonable degree of controlling behavior. But when people consult me for parenting help, the cord is usually a bit frayed, and there's not so much forgiveness available. These are the times when controlling is most costly, and ironically these are the times when it is most frequent.

Raymond, The Terrible

Raymond, a seven-year-old child, is tantrumming and throwing toys and refusing to turn off the television at bedtime. He screams, "I hate you" and cries inconsolably. His parents, Ray senior and Molly, say, "He's out of control," which really means that they can't find an effective way to respond. It's actually their world that's out of control—there's imbalance between what they want and what they have. This lack of balance generates all kinds of behavior aimed at restoring their sense of inner control as capable, caring parents. They set limits, they scold, they time out, they punish—they try everything but aren't able to change their son's miserable behavior.

This is a pretty tough and very common situation that we face as parents. Even if your child doesn't use tantrums as a "disruption of choice," he's got some favorite response that leaves you feeling frustrated, powerless, and way out of balance. We'll come back to this family in a bit and try to help Ray and Molly develop an effective parenting choice. As a first step though, it would be helpful if they understood something about "the three C's."

The Three C's

When our children choose behavior that is at odds with our picture of what we want from them, our worlds are out of balance. We know it immediately because we feel some kind of distress, perhaps anxiety or annoyance. The control imperative dictates that we generate some response that will restore balance and our sense of inner control. All too often the response that parents choose is a control maneuver. True to the external psychology of our culture, we instinctively pressure our children to change their behavior. The most common control maneuvers are *criticism, correction, and coercion*, the three C's. They are the surest ways for parents to damage the connection with their children.

Some commonly used criticism:

> *"What's the matter with you…I can't believe you did that…What were you thinking?…That's ridiculous…You've got to be kidding!"*

Some commonly used correction:

> *"No, no, don't do it that way…That isn't right, go back and do it again…No, you're wrong, I'll tell you how it happened…Oh, I have a much better outfit for you to wear to the party."*

Some commonly used coercion:

> *"Do that again and it'll be the last time we come to the park…Clean you room today or there's no play date this weekend…Get home on time or you're grounded!"*

Oh, by the way, this is also coercive:

> *"I'll give you twenty bucks for every "A" on your next report card."*

Control Maneuver Inventory

Take a moment to write a few of your favorite control maneuvers:

	IN WHAT WAYs DO I…	HOW OFTEN…	HOW UPSETTING…
SAMPLE CRITICISE	"You're always leaving your things around; can't you ever pick up after yourself?"	Certainly daily; often several times each day.	I think it is pretty upsetting to my son.
CRITICISE ("That's not very good.")			
CORRECT ("This is a much better way.")			
COERCE ("You'd better do this!")			

Don't be too hard on yourself; we all use control maneuvers when we can't find a more effective response. With greater awareness, you might find a gap between the parenting picture that you want, and the reality of your current behavior. What do you think? _____
_____.

> *Ray and Molly have used all of the three C's in their effort to stop little Raymond's tantrums. They've angrily told him that good boys don't act that way; Ray has threatened to take privileges away if his son didn't stop screaming; Molly has offered him treats such as a new Nintendo game if he'd just cooperate with the baby sitter. Though they differ in their approaches, they are both locked into an external control psychology, pressuring their child to change his behavior. Surely they've got to intervene. Wouldn't it be irresponsible to let him "get away with" his frequent tantrums? So what is so wrong with this control psychology?*

Control Parenting:
My job is to make sure my child makes good choices.

Choice Parenting
My job is to help my child learn to make good choices.

The main problem with an external, coercive approach is that it doesn't produce what you want most. At any given moment, a control maneuver might do just that—control behavior. If they use a big enough carrot or stick, Molly and Ray can probably get Raymond to quiet down. What they won't get is Raymond to become interested in changing his pattern of problem behavior, and that's really what they want most. After all, our goal as parents is not to raise compliant children. Our goal is to raise competent, creative children—children who can generate plans, accurately evaluate their choices, and improve upon them when they aren't working. Raymond isn't interested in working with his parents to solve this family problem because their control maneuvers are disconnecting. Their efforts haven't encouraged Raymond to join them; they've only encouraged him to run for cover.

"Today's Kids Need a Swift Kick in the Butt"

Many people complain that our culture has become too permissive. They say that kids have too much freedom, and that parents are reluctant to "put their foot down." Of course there's truth to the position that many parents are far too lenient. They make few demands on their children in terms of responsibility to the family, and as a result their children feel entitled to enjoy privilege and self-indulgence without limits. Eventually, the behavior becomes so irritating that the parent pushes back, hard. In my experience, most "indulgent" parents periodically lash out with a rather harsh intervention, be it screaming, hitting, or punishing. This explosive expression of power might shake up the child and lead him to change some behavior. He might even be more helpful or polite for a short time, but rarely does a swift kick lead to lasting improvement.

The highly controlling imposition of parental power is very disconnecting, and because of that, it rarely helps the child become more self aware or responsible. Nonetheless, the power play is satisfying to parents for two reasons: 1) there is often a brief change in the child's behavior—he may be temporarily more compliant, and 2) the expression of power allows parents to regain a sense of inner control—they feel as though they've done something, when something certainly needed to be done.

Rather than putting their foot down hard, lenient parents need to move their feet—and become more involved with their children. The kind of involvement that I'm talking about includes limits, expectations, and discussions about family responsibility. **The delicate balance of parenting requires being involved without being controlling.** Choice psychology gives us a game plan for how to do just that. Follow this game plan, and you can maintain a sense of inner control, even when your child is struggling with difficult and confusing behavior.

4. CHOICE PSYCHOLOGY: A Better Way To Live

The only thing any of us can control is our own behavior. That simple truth is the heart of choice psychology. Perhaps it seems obvious to you. After all, you've lived through the '70s and know all about empowerment. We're responsible for our actions—what's new and different about that? The truth is, we may talk a good game, but we live according to the customs of the external control world around us. It guides the way many of us parent, especially when we're struggling with children with challenging temperament and behavior. And when we parent with external control, we pass that psychology on to our children. Fortunately, there really is a better way.

Here's a very simple example about limit setting, just to give you a flavor of what I'm talking about. Everyone understands that good parenting involves limits, but what is it exactly that we're limiting? Most of us think about limiting our child's behavior, which is the wrong idea.

> You tell your six-year-old she can only have one cookie, and when she begins to "test the limits," you show her that you have the power to prevent her from getting that second cookie. This is classic external control thinking. Now this is not really a terrible response; it's unlikely to be damaging even if it is based on a flawed psychology. She might sulk a bit, and she may even learn not to sneak extra cookies—while you're around.

> What you could try, however, is to be clear about the limits of your own behavior, because that's the only thing you have any real control over. Everything else is a thinly veiled threat. Tell your daughter that you only want her to have one cookie, and when she puts up a stink, tell her that you really mean it—you only want her to have one. Then walk away and let her work it out.

> That's real limit setting—you've told her what <u>your</u> limit is. Will she take advantage? Maybe, in the short run. Of course, if she continually chooses to disregard your limits, you'll have other choices to make, choices that might include fewer trips to the snack aisle at the grocery store. This is not the same as saying, "take another cookie, and it'll be your last!" That's a threat, and with it you insist on controlling her behavior at that moment. It's much better to let her know what you consider acceptable and let her experience her own choice. Over time, a child who is parented this way is more capable, more connected, and more motivated to cooperate.

The simple statement at the head of this chapter,

"The only thing any of us can control is our own behavior,"

is really shorthand for the three essential elements that define choice psychology.

First, unless we resort to pure physical force, we don't control what others do. We choose our behavior, and they choose theirs. This is the element of *internal control*. Second, the behavior that we're all choosing isn't limited to the overt physical stuff. There are all kinds of internal, covert responses that we choose as well—thoughts, feelings, and even some physiology. This is the element of *total behavior*. And third, we choose behavior for reasons that make good sense to us. We never set out to screw things up; we're always trying our best to meet basic psychological needs. This is the element of *best attempt*.

> ## *Three Elements of Choice Psychology*
>
> *1) Internal Control*
>
> *2) Total Behavior*
>
> *3) Best Attempt*

The three elements that I'm about to describe are the guideposts of this different way of thinking about parenting. Choice psychology provides a game plan, a general strategy that will guide the interventions that you make. There's plenty of information available about child rearing, child management, and parenting techniques. Many of the techniques are reasonable and well researched. In my experience, though, the mindset and attitude behind the intervention is every bit as important as the intervention itself. A "time out" can be experienced by a child as a very punitive measure or as a tough but fair consequence. So much of that experience is colored by the attitude and tone of the parent. With a good understanding of choice psychology, a parent has a clear and consistent approach to his child's most challenging behavior. Interventions are more successful because they are applied with confidence and a sense of purpose. We're trying to help our children learn to evaluate their own behavior and make more successful, satisfying choices.

The First Element: Internal Control

We're responsible for what we do. If we really accept the idea that we choose our behavior and generate our emotional responses, then we won't waste time and energy making excuses. So many consistently blame their mistakes, difficulties and transgressions on external circumstance that it's become an acceptable way to operate. People say, *"I couldn't help being late, I got held up by traffic."* Or, *"This job of mine is driving me crazy."* Well, that doesn't seem so unreasonable—it's just a shorthand way of speaking, right? Maybe, but external psychology is so imbedded in the culture that it extends to more serious situations, such as, *"My daughter can't really do well in school because of her learning disability,"* and, *"My son makes me so mad; sometimes I can't help but scream at him."*

When your son blames you for his unhappiness or tells you that you "have to" drive him back to school to look for the baseball glove he left behind, there is a denial of the first element at work. When you blame your daughter for creating so much stress in the family or tell her that she "has to" do a better job of picking up her room, you are also ignoring the reality that she "has to" do nothing of the sort. She'll always choose to do what makes sense to her, regardless of how intensively you tell her that she has no choice.

People who understand and are honest with themselves about the first element are easy to spot. They say things like, "Sorry I'm late; I didn't expect so much traffic. I'll leave more time in the future." And more importantly, "My son is really difficult for me to handle; I'm not happy about the way I've been screaming at him." They understand that to deny their essential responsibility for their own behavior will do nothing to improve things and to accept external excuses for their children's behavior will only enable their dependence and limited self worth.

We're not just talking about a difference in language here. In the examples cited above the difference between the control and the choice parents is that they think about the situation differently, that's why the words come out differently. Sometimes the language may be the same but the tone is completely different. Think of how many ways there are to ask, "Why didn't you call us?"

It's very common for people to blame current difficulties on past events. A difficult childhood is often cited as the reason for someone's unbalanced life today. This is classic external control thinking, and a misguided point of view. Yes, it's important to recognize and understand the past, but it is essential to acknowledge that the past doesn't continue to determine our present behavior. I see many divorced parents who feel terrible about what they've put their children through, and so they lower their expectations for their children's conduct, hoping not to add to their already burdensome life. The wrong assumption here is that a difficult history causes a difficult present, and that the children are not capable of managing their current circumstances. "Yes," I tell them, "he's had a difficult time; and yes, he's still responsible for getting his homework done." He can do it if he chooses to, regardless of the past. He'll need understanding and support, but he can learn to manage his life effectively.

THINK IT OVER, WRITE IT DOWN…

When have you accepted responsibility for a problem or difficulty, rather than blaming it on external causes?

_____

_____

_____

Another consequence of our prevailing external psychology is the proliferation of childhood psychiatric disorders. There's LD, ADHD, OCD, ODD, and the list goes on. When I meet one of these kids who have been given a bunch of these diagnoses, I like to say with a friendly smile, "Oh, a man of letters!" These children quickly understand my little joke and are usually relieved to find a professional who doesn't buy into "disability doom." They and their parents find out soon enough what the choice psychology perspective is—that a child may have some skill weaknesses that are not his fault, but he is quite capable of finding ways to meet his academic and social responsibilities. He'll never choose to work hard in school if he's told that because of a disability he can't succeed. So think twice before you petition the school district to reduce your daughter's summer reading load. Get all the special support you're entitled to, but don't lower the expectation of what she can achieve because of a so-called "disability." Thousands of kids with skill weaknesses do well in school, and in life, when they so choose.

The Second Element: Total Behavior

When we choose a behavior, such as going out for a run, we're generating more than the physical action of moving our body along at a fast pace. We're also thinking about a route, feeling pleased about ourselves for finally getting off our butts, and even changing the physiology of our heart rate and respiration. We're not simply choosing to run, but we're choosing the total behavior of exercise. Everything we do, every behavior we choose, actually occurs as a complex of responses on four distinct levels. There is the overt physical activity called *acting*, the covert mental activity called *thinking*, the emotional activity called *feeling*, and the physiological activity called *physiology*. Together these four components make up the complex called *total behavior*.

We always choose total behavior, because **all behavior is total behavior**. It always occurs as a complex.

Here's where the word "choice" gets a bit tricky, because we think of a choice as something we have a great deal of conscious control over. It's pretty clear that while we have a lot of direct control over running, our control over respiration and cardiovascular activity is less direct.

Think of total behavior as a suitcase (Wubbolding, 1991):

ACTING	THINKING
FEELING	PHYSIOLOGY

You can't pick up just a piece of the suitcase. When you grab the handle, the rest of it comes right along. It's much the same with total behavior. When you yell (an action) with anger at your child, the thinking, feeling, and physiology of "being angry" comes right along with it. We might say then that when you choose to yell, you also choose anger, and perhaps an upset stomach. The anger doesn't just happen to you—it's part of the total behavior that you've chosen.

The handle on the top of the suitcase represents the direct control that we have over these various parts of behavior. It is connected to the acting and thinking parts, because we have the most control over them. We can consciously and deliberately choose our actions; most people would agree with that. We also have quite a bit of control over thinking behavior as well. It's true; there are troublesome thoughts that seem to pop into our minds of their own accord. Once they are recognized, however, we can decide to strengthen them with plenty of attention or to shift our mental focus in another direction. We can decide to give someone the benefit of the doubt or to view him as a conniving scoundrel. We have quite a bit of direct control over our actions and our thoughts, and therefore it makes sense to call them "chosen behaviors."

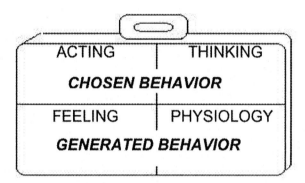

We have less direct control over our emotional and physiological life, and so you might prefer to consider them "generated behaviors," but the internal control is there nonetheless. I know that when I play tennis with my son I usually feel happy and proud. Is <u>he</u> making me feel happy? Is the <u>tennis game</u> making me feel happy? Actually, it's neither. I'm choosing my own happiness when I choose the total behavior of "tennis with my son."

I also know that I can generate, or "choose," a mildly depressed mood by avoiding paperwork and other tedious pieces of business for too long. When I'm in this funk, it would be easy for me to tell myself that I'm putting off the work because I'm feeling a bit down. The truth of the matter is that both of these behaviors—procrastinating and feeling down—are parts of the same total behavior of "being depressed." From a choice psychology perspective, I'm choosing my own distress.

There are physiological responses that are automatic; some people are just born moodier than others, some tend to be more anxious. These inborn response sets are called *temperament*, but they don't altogether determine how we act and feel. Even temperament can be modified by purposeful changes in thought and activity.

When you understand the element of *total behavior*, you begin to evaluate your own experience in a very different way. Rather than asking,

"Who's making me so upset?"

…you begin to ask,

"What is it I'm doing to generate this feeling?"
"Is it consistent with the picture that I want?"
"Can I choose a different response?"

This kind of self-evaluation is a key part of the shift to choice psychology. We'll do more of it later, but it requires a very solid understanding of total behavior.

Recognizing Your Own Total Behavior

Choose a specific problem behavior or activity of your own—something that you currently do that's unsatisfying or annoying (e.g. mowing the lawn, having lunch with a business associate, helping your son with homework…). Close your eyes for a moment, and really imagine yourself doing that activity. Write it briefly here:

_____

_____

Now, identify the Acting part. (What are you physically doing?) Write it in the top left compartment of the suitcase.

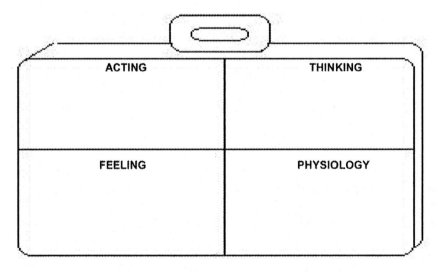

Complete the rest of the suitcase with the other parts of your total behavior:

<u>Identify the Thinking.</u> (What are you saying to yourself, in your mind, as you carry out this activity?)

<u>Identify the Feeling.</u> (How are you feeling—nervous, annoyed, impatient, joyful, sad?)

<u>Identify the Physiology.</u> (What is your body doing—heart racing, stomach churning, breathing calm, muscles relaxed?)

O.K., now close your eyes again, and imagine choosing a different action or thought—the same general "problem activity," but this time choose a new action or thought that is more consistent with a picture of the parent you'd like to be. Put it in this new suitcase:

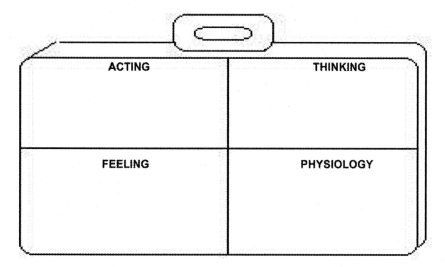

Now, fill in the other parts that will naturally follow along with this behavior. Feeling better?

Parents who understand total behavior respond to an upset child in a very different way. These parents are reluctant to view their children as a victims of some external circumstance that is causing distress, but rather understand that the upset feeling is part of a child's chosen way of coping with a difficult challenge.

Lisa is an eight year old who has trouble leaving her mother in the morning for school. She is a reluctant child by temperament and often chooses the total behavior "being nervous" which, for her, includes avoiding, pleading, and an upset stomach. Lisa's mother has been learning to use choice psychology to respond to the difficult morning behavior.

Lisa: *"Mom, can't you please drive me today—you know the bus makes my tummy hurt?"*

Mom: *"I know the bus ride is not easy for you sweetheart, but it's not convenient for me to drive you today. Is there anything else I can do to help?"*

Lisa: *"NO!!! You have to drive me, otherwise I know I'll be sick!"*

Mom: *"I sure hope you find a way to be comfortable on the bus, but I really meant it when I said that I won't be driving you. Let me know when you're ready to go to the bus stop."*

Lisa: *"O.K., O.K, but will you wait at the corner with me?"*

Mom: *"Yes, I think I have time for that. I'd be happy to wait with you."*

In many cases, the pleading would go on for a lot longer. Lisa and her mom have gone through this routine quite a few times already, and at this point Lisa chooses to calm down rather quickly in the face of her mother's resolve. What's most important here is mom's clarity about her daughter's responsibility for her own total behavior. Mom doesn't blame Lisa for being difficult, or in any way diminish the seriousness of her challenge. But neither does she excuse Lisa from her business, which is to find some way to ride the bus to school. Mom stays connected and maintains her position. This is not an easy response for a parent to make in the face of dramatic, emotional behavior. However, with a clear plan and a bit of practice, most parents can learn to do this very well.

An understanding of *total behavior* will help you get what you really want as a parent. I suggest that you seek more than order and compliance; you really want your child to evaluate his behavior and learn to make responsible choices. These objectives are the heart of choice parenting.

5. MORE CHOICE PSYCHOLOGY: We're All Doing Our Best

The Third Element: Best Attempt

No one wakes up in the morning, looks in the mirror and says, "I think I'll really screw things up today." No, we're always trying our best to get more of what we want and need, choosing behavior that we expect to be satisfying. After the fact, we may find that some of our choices were very poor ones. But in the present moment, we behave in a way that makes good sense to us.

Understanding this element is critical to responding well to your child's difficult behavior, because

> *Three Elements of Choice Psychology*
>
> *1) Internal Control*
>
> *2) Total Behavior*
>
> *3) Best Attempt*

unless your response indicates that his behavior has some reasonable rationale, he will disconnect from you. And while it's true that you might be looking for some behavior change, you most certainly do not want a disconnected child. Try to appreciate that as foolish or selfish as his behavior might seem, it made good sense to him at the time he chose it. He was simply doing what we all do, trying his best to choose satisfying behavior. He was making what seemed to him to be a reasonable attempt to gain status, or perhaps to have fun. That's what we all do, all the time. That's what all this choosing behavior is about, trying to satisfy our basic physical and psychological needs. I'll describe each of these needs a bit later, but for those of you who have difficulty waiting, here they are:

> *Survival, Love, Power, Fun, and Freedom.*

This *best attempt* element is so simple, and so important. All too often parents respond to their children's behavior with a mindset that says, "Are you crazy?" or "How could you possibly be so selfish?" This leaves them with very little chance of staying connected as they intervene. The third element suggests a different mindset. It suggests good-faith curiosity rather than skeptical criticism. Consider your response when you discover the family room in total disarray—furniture moved around, games and toys covering the floor. Your impulse might be to say,

> *"What kind of nonsense is happening here? Get this mess cleaned up right away!"*

But from the child's perspective, this isn't nonsense. This is good fun, and what's wrong with that? The only thing "wrong" is that it violates your picture of an orderly home, also a legitimate view. Here's a different way to respond when you enter that wouldn't be so disconnecting:

"Wow, it looks like you guys have been busy! What have you been up to?"

Again, it's not the words, but the fact that you begin with the assumption that something sensible is going on. Your children weren't trying to mess up the room; they were trying to have fun. Once they tell you a bit about it, you might ask if the room can get back to the way it used to be. If you use the skills that encourage a connection, you're likely to get some measure of cooperation.

The Basic Needs

We always choose behavior for the purpose of meeting one of five basic needs. These needs, *survival, power, love, freedom, and fun,* are built-in and universal. The first of these is really a biological need that we share with all living creatures that strive to maintain physical well-being and reproduce. The others are the uniquely human psychological needs. We differ from one another in the relative strength of our needs, but we all have the same ones. You might have a higher need for freedom than your husband, for example, while his need for power may be greater than yours. And while we can't change or control the basic needs that motivate us, we certainly can control our choice of specific behaviors. **We always choose total behavior that we hope will be need satisfying.**

> ## *THE BASIC NEEDS*
>
> *Survival and Physical Well-Being*
>
> *Love and Belonging*
>
> *Power and Self-Worth*
>
> *Freedom*
>
> *Fun and Learning*

The need for survival and physical well-being drives our healthy behavior. We all want to be safe and live without threat of harm or illness. Our efforts to take care of our bodies, to drive carefully, and to protect our financial assets are expressions of our innate need for survival. Hunger, thirst, and the sex drive are also part of this global need for physical well-being.

The need for love and belonging drives our social behavior. It feels good to us to be connected, to be understood, and to be thought of by others. This need also drives more intimate behavior such as family and romantic love. In all of these cases, we choose behavior that we hope will lead to more connectedness with others.

> *A young girl presses her mommy to arrange a play date. She's trying her best to meet her need for belonging.*
>
> *A young boy sulks on the playground, apart from the others. He hasn't found an effective way to belong.*
>
> *A father with a high need for love and belonging waits eagerly for each letter home from summer camp. He often chooses to think about his son.*
>
> *A frustrated mother tries new ways to "protect the cord" that connects her with her difficult teenage daughter. She's trying hard to improve their relationship.*
>
> ***Name a way that you meet your need for love and belonging:***
>
> _____
>
> _____.

The need for power, achievement and self-worth drives our productive behavior. All of our attempts to be effective, to "get ahead" and to produce quality work, derive from this need. Our interest in being the best parents we can is a specific expression of our need for achievement. When we're effective, we feel proud and worthwhile; when we're unsuccessful, we feel frustrated and our self-worth suffers.

> *A young girl feels terrific when she brings home a spelling test with a big "A" on top.*
>
> *An ambitious father works long hours, hoping to move up in the world of business.*
>
> *The playground bully teases a younger boy, hoping to feel strong and powerful.*

A young mother decides to "stay at home," and feels proud to be doing her best for the family.

Two girlfriends collect a boxful of quarters running a lemonade stand on a hot summer afternoon.

Name a way that you meet your need for power and self-worth:

_____

_____.

The need for freedom drives us to be independent, to choose our own course. When we express our points of view, create something original, or just go off by ourselves, we are satisfying our freedom need. It's because of this need that we so resent being dictated to by others. Our need to determine our own path is so fundamental that attempts by others to control us are always disconnecting.

A young boy enjoys time by himself, creating make-believe villages with building blocks.

A rebellious teenager argues with her biology teacher, insisting that science is only one way of arriving at "truth."

A concerned parent reads several books on child behavior, preferring to develop her own approach rather than depending on one expert's opinion.

Name a way that you meet your need for freedom:

_____

_____.

The need for fun and learning drives our search for discovery and our interest in play. We all know what it feels like to be having fun. The healthiest people are those who find a way to play all their lives and who bring a playful attitude to their work and their relationships. These people are fun to be with.

William Glasser is the first theorist that I know of who linked the concepts of fun and learning. From his perspective, "fun is the genetic reward for learning (1998)." In his groundbreaking work on education, he makes the important distinction between "schooling" and learning. Schooling is the external control approach to information transmission, and it isn't much fun. Walk down any school hallway and it's easy to find where real learning is taking place—listen for the laughter and look for the smiles.

Another very useful way of thinking about the basic needs has been presented by Barnes Boffey (1997). He talks about the "basic instructions" to survive, to be loving, to be powerful, to be free, and to be playful. We have no choice but to follow these general instructions, but we have tremendous freedom to choose our own way to carry out those instructions.

THINK IT OVER, WRITE IT DOWN...

When your child is frustrated or upset, what is the basic need that he/she seems to have a hard time satisfying?

_____

_____

_____.

So Now You Know...

With choice psychology, you have a new way of thinking about your child's irresponsible, self-defeating, or disruptive behavior. You can see that the behavior is chosen—that is, it is not determined by some external disorder or circumstance that is completely outside of his control. You can also appreciate that the problem behavior makes sense; it represents your child's current best attempt to meet basic psychological needs. By the same token, you've been choosing behavior in an effort to be an effective parent. You, too, have been making your current best attempt. It's quite likely that you've been guided by a control psychology and have been blaming your child for bad behavior, pressuring him to act more responsibly or chastising yourself for being such a lousy parent. But if you can truly view your and your child's behavior through this new lens of choice psychology, you will discover quite a different way of responding. Your new best attempt will create the connection that you want, and that your child needs in order to live a responsible and fulfilling life.

6. THE PARENT SELF-EVALUATION: Creating a Picture of the Parent You Want to Be

It isn't easy to change your total parenting behavior. As you make the transition from a reliance on external control to the use of more choice psychology, it will be helpful for you to have a picture in your mind of your goal. A clear vision of yourself being the parent you'd most like to be can sustain you during the rough times—the times when your child is relying on control maneuvers. As you choose not to take the bait, you can call upon that picture and use it to help you retain a sense of inner control. Even when the world doesn't cooperate, you can always feel somewhat satisfied that you're carrying out your own plan.

Barnes Boffey (1997) has an elegant way of helping people self-evaluate and create this kind of "unifying vision." He has them ask themselves:

> *If I had the courage to be the person I wanted to be, how would I handle my present situation?*

After visualizing an answer to that question, Boffey suggests that they act as if they were that person. This is consistent with the element of total behavior that says if we "act as if," the rest of the suitcase will follow. That is, we'll soon think, feel and physically respond as if we were the person we'd most like to be.

Parent Self-Evaluation

Take a few moments and think about the following questions. I suggest that you slow down, take a breath, and consider them one at a time:

> *If I had the courage to be the parent I want to be, how might I act differently?*

> *If I had the courage to be the parent I want to be, what might I be thinking?*

> *If I had the courage to be the parent I want to be, how might I be feeling?*

> *If I had the courage to be the parent I want to be, how might my body be responding?*

Now close your eyes and create a picture of yourself as the parent you want to be. Use your answers to the previous total behavior questions to help you form your

32

vision. Make it as specific as possible; imagine how you're dressed and details of the physical surroundings.

> *VISUALIZE the parent you want to be.*

Now, after you've created a clear, unifying vision of the parent you want to be, take a step closer to being that parent. Using that picture as a guide, identify something that you would be willing to do differently, right away, that you believe would make you a better parent—something that will improve your relationship with your child.

Keep the following guidelines in mind as you select your new behavior:
- BE REALISTIC. The step you select should be simple and within your grasp; chose something you're sure you can do.
- BE UNCONDITIONAL. Resolve to chose this new behavior <u>regard-less</u> of how others behave—not "only if" they do this or that.
- BE COMMITTED. Be clear that you <u>will</u> do this—not that you'll try or intend to.

Now, state exactly what it is that you will do differently—right away.

> *To be more of the parent I want to be, I will*
>
> _____
>
> _____
>
> _____.

The exercise you just completed is a special kind of self-evaluation. Any time you reflect on your own behavior and ask how well it's working, or what you might do differently in order to achieve a better result, you're self-evaluating. This is an important part of choice parenting because it is essential for meaningful behavior change. You can read as many instructive parenting books as you like, but unless you reflect on your own behavior and compare it to an idea of what you really want, you will never be motivated to substantially change your own behavior.

There is a parallel process at work in this book. Just as you are evaluating your behavior, you'll soon be encouraging your child to do the same. This is certainly what I want most for my children—for them to be aware and evaluate their own actions and choices. With the control psychology of threats and punishment, you only encourage your child to comply or be sneaky. With a choice psychology of connection and self-evaluation, your child learns to make more effective choices that satisfy a broader range of needs.

The Parent's Paradox

One of the most important lessons of choice psychology is that external control is disconnecting. But we also know that responsible parents sometimes need to be controlling. Is there a contradiction here? Of course there is, and it's why effective parenting involves a paradox. There's no perfect solution for this riddle; everyone has to find his or her own way.

I was working with a successful physician who had a very unhappy teenage son. The boy was choosing a lot of oppositional and defiant behavior, some of which was dangerous. As his dad learned about choice psychology, he struggled mightily with the parent's paradox. In one of our conversations, he explained his own resolution this way:

> *I think of punishment in the same way I think of cortisone. It's a powerful substance that can do a lot of damage, but sometimes the patient needs it. I prescribe it very judiciously.*

Choice psychology does not imply that you should never choose controlling behavior. It only explains that there is always a cost, and that you should try hard to avoid it. Of course you have to prevent physical harm and injury, but when you become committed to responding with choice, you'll find that the circumstances that actually require control are few and far between.

To, For, and With

Dr. William Glasser, the author of Choice Theory, tells us there are three ways we can relate to our children (1984). We can do things to them, we can do things for them, and we can do things with them. The first two, he says, are of little value.

In a way, this book is all about overcoming the controlling impulse to do things to and for our children, and instead to create new ways to do things with them. This is especially challenging when discipline is called for, but it can be done. The "toolbox" section will offer some specific ideas.

Punishment and the use of the *three C's (criticism, correction, coercion)* are the most frequent ways in which we do things *to* our children. We have good reason; we're trying to provide guidance. We're satisfying our power need to be effective and responsible parents. Sadly, our children's experience of these encounters is more upsetting than we may realize. They feel oppressed, controlled, and inhibited. To regain their emotional balance they might push back by being oppositional, or shut down by being sullen and self-critical. In either case, our goal of guiding our children toward more responsible behavior is not well met.

> *Steve, a divorced dad, consulted me on the advice of his son's school counselor. His ten-year-old son, Jackie, recently came to live with him after a protracted custody battle. After only a few weeks of school, Jackie was in trouble with his teachers. He wasn't paying attention, was rude to the teachers, and often played with his "Game-Boy" during class despite frequent corrections. He would promise to leave the game at home, but continue to sneak it into class.*

> *"The worst part about it is that he lies," his dad explained to me. "He lies to the teacher, the principal, and then comes home and lies to me. He says they're out to get him—that he wasn't even playing with the game. He never owns up to his mistakes. The last time I grounded him for a week. This time, I took the Game-Boy away."*

> *Of course I asked Steve if he found these penalties to be effective, and he regretfully acknowledged that they were not. "He's always totally outraged—like he's been falsely accused again. He says terrible things to me, and I'll admit that I scream right back at him. Eventually, he's full of apologies, but it feels like he's just trying to get me to end the punishment. In the end, nothing changes. We've been through this so many times, you'd think he'd learn."*

> *Steve's punishing approach is a common way of responding to irresponsible behavior, and a perfect example of intervening by doing <u>to</u> your child. His son is already pretty disengaged, avoiding classroom involvement and attempting to deceive the adults around him. Punishment is unlikely to encourage better engagement. In the "toolbox" section that follows, we'll see how Steve applies a new approach to his son's difficulties. He uses the "on hold" method to solve the problem <u>with</u> his son, and improves the connection between them to boot!*

We love our children, and it's uncomfortable to see them struggle, so we're also apt to do far too much *for* them. It's often more convenient, especially with very young children, to do things for them. Every mother knows that picking up a child's room for her is quicker and easier than doing it with her. Nonetheless, the cost of parental over-functioning is high. There is a risk of encouraging an entitled attitude whereby your child believes it is unreasonable to be uncomfortable and unnecessary to work hard. An emotionally entitled child actually thinks of herself as incapable of overcoming challenges and obstacles, and this lack of confidence is the bedrock of poor self-esteem. In fact, this is one of the biggest parenting problems faced by affluent families—the development of an emotionally entitled child. An important key is to try, whenever possible, to change your *doing to* and *doing for*, to *doing with*. By way of example, let's talk for a moment about homework.

So many parents struggle with their children over homework. This shouldn't be surprising, as homework represents the first substantial independent responsibility for many children. Some adjust to the duty with little difficulty, while others struggle mightily. If they are resistant, a concerned parent has to choose how to be involved.

> *Adam is an eight year old who's had difficulty being successful in math. His older sister is quite proficient, and he's decided that he "can't do math." He invites his mother's involvement in his homework by pouting and complaining. "I can't do this…I'm too stupid to do this." His mom employs her best choice psychology, and responds, "You seem very unhappy. Anything I can do to help?" "No," he replies, "there's nothing you can do. I'll never be able to do this. Its too hard." "Well, let me know if you'd like me to look at it with you," she responds. "I'm sure we can make some sense out of it together."*

> *At this point she keeps her distance, but doesn't disappear. Having made the offer, she's demonstrated a genuine willingness to help, but maintains clearly that it's <u>his</u> homework. In this case, after five or ten minutes of pouting, Adam accepts the offer.*

> *"O.K. mom, will you look at it with me?"*

> *Mom understands that this is only the first hurdle and fully expects Adam to continue to resist responsibility by complaining and insisting that his mother provide the answer for him. Here are a few more of the exchanges between them:*

Adam: "*There's just too many of them, and they're way too hard for me. Can't you do a few of them?*"

Mom: "*I know it looks like a lot. Why don't you just pick one for now that you think you can do?*"

Adam: "*That's it—I've had enough. I can't do anymore.*"

Mom: "*Well, you put in a good effort on that one. Maybe you should take a break? Don't forget though, no T.V. 'til it's all done.*"

Adam: "*I have no idea how to do this. You'll have to do it.*"

Mom: "*Tell you what—let's do one together, and we'll stay with it 'til you really understand it.*"

This mom is a pro at doing homework with her son, rather than for him. She also avoids the to him trap by staying available and involved rather than simply insisting that he get it done, and leaving him with no support. The balancing act that she's performing is her own skillful way of handling the parent paradox; she's doing her best to parent by choice.

What You Want Most

Because we have multiple basic needs, we often want different things at the same time. You might, for example, want to take a Saturday to go off alone and do some fishing (fun, freedom). At the same time, you might want to watch you kids' soccer games (love and belonging). The most common of these inner conflicts for parents are between power and belonging. We want to be effective parents, directing our children to make proper choices and making sure that they live responsibly. That's our power instruction compelling us to be the best parents we can. But we also want to enjoy our relationship with our children, to simply let them be who they are, and to feel connected with them. That's our love and belonging instruction, pushing us to care and to enjoy being a family.

The conflict between power and belonging comes up all the time for us as parents—every time we feel the need to correct or control our children. You might ask yourself…

"*How much will this criticism impair the connection with my daughter?*"

"Is it so important that I correct my son, that I'm willing to create dishar-mony?"

In reality, the challenge is not so much to choose <u>between</u> power and belonging, but to successfully integrate the two—to be an effectively involved parent. The goal is to intervene in a way that maintains the connection. That is really the art of choice parenting.

I don't think that I'm promoting a particularly lenient approach. I would never advocate, for example, that parents avoid giving unwelcome news to their children in order to protect their connection. Saying "no," and setting limits are essential parts of any honest and satisfying relationship. Refusing your daughter's request for a ride to the video store, after she spent much of the day promising yet failing to help you with the yard work, is not a disconnecting response. You don't much feel like taking her, and that's a good reason to say "no." However, if you were to say, "No, and how selfish of you to even ask," that would indeed be disconnecting.

Now it may be difficult to bite your tongue and forego the critical response when you believe that your daughter has been selfish.

"Isn't it important that she be told?"
"Shouldn't she be corrected?"
"If I forego the criticism, am I not enabling the development of rotten, spoiled kid?"

No, no, and no! Believe me, she'll figure it out. You're not taking her to the store because you don't want to, and that naturally occurring consequence is powerful enough without trumping it up with a punishing statement like, "that's what happens when you treat people the way you do."

This is where it is helpful to ask yourself two important self-evaluating questions:

"What do I want?"
and, *"What do I want most?"*

You may *want* to point out how irresponsibly you daughter's been behaving, but what you want *most* is for her to develop her own sense of responsibility. That kind of moral and emotional development is best achieved through an honest relationship with someone she cares about. I hope that's you! If you keep in mind that picture of the parent you what to be, you'll bite your tongue and protect the connection.

SECTION TWO
A BETTER SET OF TOOLS

7. THE OLD TOOLS: Reinforcement, Punishment, and Time Out

This begins the "how to" section of the book. Five new tools or techniques will be presented that are based on the choice psychology that we've been discussing. They will help you respond to challenging behavior while maintaining an emotional connection with your child. In each case, your response will accomplish two important things. First, you'll clearly let your child know that his behavior is somehow problematic for you. And second, you'll encourage your child to self-evaluate. This is what you want most, even more than a change in the particular behavior that you're upset about. What you want most is for your child to routinely evaluate the effectiveness of his behavior.

The five new tools, *stay connected, encourage self-evaluation, set your limits, plan together,* and *put specials on hold* are presented in order from the simplest to the most complex. In practice, these tools are not so distinct from one another—each builds upon the one that precedes it. You can blend them in any way that seems sensible to you.

Before these new tools are presented in the chapters that follow, we'll briefly review the old ones; the stalwarts that everyone is so familiar with, *reinforcement, punishment, and time out.* They're embraced by many parents and professionals, and with good reason, for each offers something satisfying. With the perspective of choice psychology though, we'll see that we can really do much better.

Reinforcement

Danny's father gives him ten dollars for every "A" on his report card.

39

Sarah has a "star chart" on the refrigerator that records mornings she woke up with a dry bed.

Ben's Mom told him that if he helps out with the snow shoveling, he'll be allowed to sleep over his friend's house this weekend.

Positive reinforcement is widely touted as the intervention of choice to modify behavior. It's summarized in the following advice given to me during my graduate training at a child behavior clinic:

"Catch them being good, then reinforce the hell out of 'em!"

Strictly speaking, reinforcement means:

…introducing a consequence that increases the frequency of the behavior that preceded it.

Any time we use rewards, incentives, or bribes in order to increase behavior, we're using reinforcement. What can be so bad about such a positive approach?

The problem is that the process is so external. The child who is rewarded for A's on his report card has learned that he can please his father by getting an A. Dad doesn't appear all that interested in how his son got the A's—what was helpful or what might be needed in order to continue his success. Instead, the message from Dad is like the Nike commercial—*Just Do It!*

The use of rewards and incentives requires very little involvement on the part of the parent, and perhaps that's the appeal. You can feel as though you're doing your job, and put in very little effort.

Involvement costs effort, but it pays off in belonging.

I'm not totally against the use of reinforcement, by the way. I think it's a wonderful idea for a Dad and his son to go out together and celebrate that great report card. While they're out, Dad would be wise to ask with real interest about his son's secrets of success. That kind of involvement will foster self-awareness, and continued success.

> # *REINFORCEMENT*
>
> *+ Easy To Use*
>
> *+ Pleases the Child*
>
> *- Doesn't Encourage Parent-Child Involvement*
>
> *- Doesn't Encourage Creative Problem Solving*

I'm also a big fan of star charts with young children, but only when it's their idea. Consider the following exchange:

Mom: *"You know Sarah, we've got to find a better way to help you with your bed-wetting."*

Sarah: *"It's not my fault; I really am trying my best."*

Mom: *"I know sweetheart, and you're doing a good job helping me change the sheets when they're wet. Is there anything else that might help?"*

Sarah: *"Could I get a special prize if I do very well?"*

Mom: *"Sure, if you think that will help you; it sounds like a great idea. How should we keep track?"*

Now the chart belongs to Sarah; it's part of her effort to solve a difficult problem. It doesn't feel like something that's being done to her, but something she and her mom are doing together.

In his groundbreaking book <u>Punished By Rewards</u> (1993), Alfie Kohn sums up the limitation of the use of reinforcement this way:

> *"Do rewards motivate people? Absolutely. They motivate people to get rewards."*

Punishment

The idea that your child should be punished when he misbehaves is so imbedded in our culture, that it's difficult to evaluate objectively. But we'll try. First of all, let's define the term. Punishment means:

...introducing a consequence that decreases the frequency of the behavior that precedes it.

The proverbial child curses, and his mother washes his mouth out with soap. He will stop cursing, at least in her presence. But therein lies the first of two major problems with punishment. It has a very narrow band of effectiveness. It can have a powerful effect on the very specific behavior at hand, but that's far from what a choice parent wants most. As we've said so many times, we want to encourage our children to evaluate their behaviors and correct them to more effective choices—choices that better satisfy their basic needs. Much like reinforcement, punishment is a very external experience. It does little to encourage reflection or self-examination.

The second major problem with punishment is the impact on the relationship. It's terribly disconnecting. We're often unhappy with our kids' behavior because it seems selfish—lacking consideration for others. A punishment will not encourage the child to be more generous in his attitude toward the family.

Many a dad delivers a stiff sanction, like grounding his daughter for three weeks, and then thinks to himself, "that'll give her something to think about." But what his daughter is probably thinking about is what a jerk her dad is being. She is surely not thinking about more effective alternatives to meet her pressing need for freedom.

Of course the most common punishment is the yelling and screaming that parents find themselves engaged in. Usually they regret it. They intuitively know that this is not the parent they want to be, and yet it's such a compelling choice. Why?

PUNISHMENT

+ Dramatic impact on Behavior

+ Parent Feels Powerful, In Control

- Narrow Band of Effect

- Damages Relationship

- Doesn't Encourage Creative Problem Solving

When your child defies you, your need for power is frustrated. You want badly to feel like an effective parent, and it seems as though your child is preventing you from doing so. When you yell and scream and generally act angry, you use your power to dominate, and this is marginally satisfying. You do feel powerful, but also disappointed with yourself. You probably ask, *"Is this the best response I can come up with?"* Of course not; you can definitely do better.

The error in your thinking is that your child is preventing you from being effective. It's better to evaluate your effectiveness in terms that you can control, rather than by how effectively you're controlling your child. If you intervene with a defiant child and evaluate your effort in terms of how well <u>you</u> do in the encounter— how effectively you carry out your plan—then you'll find no need to yell and scream. The new tools will help a great deal. You can feel effective regardless of how your child responds—you'll know that you did the best you could.

Time Out

Now here's a really interesting case. This old tool is still one of the most popular today, in both classrooms and family homes. Kids have been sent to their rooms or told to go sit in the corner for a long, long time. Is that time out? The answer is, maybe. A lot depends upon the tone and intention of the intervention. Time out can be a very effective tool. The problem is, what passes for time out is usually punishment in disguise.

The technique called "time out" began as a classroom intervention to manage children who had become overly stimulated by the class environment. The theory was that the disruptive behavior was being reinforced by the attention of the children's peers, and so a "time out from reinforcement" was needed. A neutral space was designated, not as a punishment, but as a place to cool out and prepare to return to the class. The teacher would use a neutral emotional tone to direct the excited child to take a brief time out. One minute for each year of age is a useful rule of thumb. When properly introduced and applied, some children actually requested a time out when they realized they were having difficulty regaining their composure. O.K., so how closely does your time out resemble that?

It's best to respond to ongoing behavior problems in a thoughtful way, at some time other than the heat of the moment. This is the only way to establish a real time out procedure, such as described by the *planning* tool in Chapter 9. Sometimes though, we're needed for crisis intervention. When a child is hurting someone or something, you may want to interrupt the behavior that's in progress.

Time out can be a great option for this situation, but only if the groundwork has been laid. Otherwise, using your power to stop behavior is basically a control maneuver. Now don't get me wrong—it may be the best choice available. When children are using violence or aggression to get their way, it's important to stop the behavior as quickly as possible. The same is true if a young child is doing something reckless or dangerous. Just be honest with yourself that when you aggressively send them to their room, you are choosing a control maneuver. As you learn the new tools of choice parenting, you'll have more options and won't have to rely primarily on external control parenting.

8. STAY CONNECTED: Working With Your Child's Temperament (including ADHD!)

Finding a way to stay connected with your child is the foundation for all of your parenting interventions. When you're totally stumped and have no idea what to do, you can never go wrong with this tool. It's a very simple idea, although not always so easy to do. Talk with your child about the issue at hand, and make the idea of staying connected your top priority. That means staying connected is more important than teaching him a lesson, getting your point across, or making sure he never does it again. Sure, you have important things to tell him, just make that part of your intervention secondary. The

THE NEW TOOLS
1. Stay Connected
2. Encourage Self-Evaluation
3. Set Your Limits
4. Plan Together
5. Put Specials On Hold

primary part is doing the best you can to stay connected in the conversation.

> *Let your child know you have a problem with his behavior, and then listen hard and bite your tongue!*

One thing that makes this simple technique so difficult is that you probably don't feel like working to stay connected after your kid just acted very selfishly. Try it anyway. The payoff for you will be the satisfaction that you feel in carrying out your plan effectively, even if your kid doesn't cooperate. Remember, it's best to evaluate your effectiveness in terms that you control. You can be the parent you want to be, even if your child is being a pain in the butt.

So how exactly do you do this—what are the best ways to stay connected? For a start, you might want to review the three C's from Chapter 3, as they are the most common ways that people *disconnect*. If you can avoid *criticizing*, *correcting*, and *coercing*, then you stand a very good chance of staying connected. So what's left? What is it that you can try to do more of that will strengthen the connection? You might try *listening*, *accepting*, and *encouraging*, which are very connecting behaviors. *Listen* to what he has to say. Even if you've heard it before, or it makes no sense to you, show him the respect of hearing him out. *Accept* his point of view as legitimate. Even if you disagree, his opinion makes sense to him. Again, respect is very connecting. *Encourage* him to stay in the conversation with you—try to discuss things in a reasonable way. A big part of choice parenting is the confidence that you convey to your child that he has the inner resources to do quality work and to relate in a connected way. Show your child how it's done!

Disconnecting Behavior	*Connecting Behavior*
Criticizing	*Listening*
Correcting	*Accepting*
Coercing	*Encouraging*
Blaming	*Trusting*
Threatening	*Respecting*
Punishing	*Negotiating*

See the Sense in his Behavior

A powerful way to stay connected is to recognize the sense in your child's behavior, even when it appears to be unreasonable. Good counselors are skilled at this technique, which is based on the third element of choice psychology (Chapter 4), *Best Attempt*. Remember that your child's problematic behavior is his best attempt to meet one or more of his basic needs. As you listen to him, try to understand which need he was trying to satisfy—*power, love, freedom or fun*. Convey to him that you understand what he wants and that you appreciate the legitimacy of his desire. That doesn't mean that you approve of his choice, but it does mean that you understand him.

> *Child: "I <u>know</u> it's late, so what! I've got to work out this solo."*
> *Parent: "You really want to be the best guitar player that you can." (power)*
>
> *Child: "I don't care how cold it is; I'm not wearing that stupid coat!"*
> *Parent: "You've got your own ideas about how to dress." (freedom)*
>
> *Child: "It wasn't my fault—the dog ran in and knocked the paint over."*
> *Parent: "I know you girls were having a lot of fun down there." (fun)*

In each of these responses, the parent has referred to the child's desire and best attempt in a respectful way—free from criticism or ridicule. It doesn't mean that the parent intends to back down or excuse careless behavior. The idea is to stay connected and keep the conversation going until some kind of understanding is reached. Acknowledging that it's reasonable for your child to want what he wants is an excellent way to stay connected. Perhaps you see his desire as unreasonable.

That's probably because you've got a different basic need in mind than he has. Parents often think about health and safety (survival/physical well-being), while children think about freedom and social status (power/self-worth). If you criticize your child's wants, you'll get nowhere. Try hard to find the sense—the best attempt—in your child's apparently unreasonable behavior.

Temperament

All children are not created equal. If you have more than one, you know this fact of child development well. Just as kids are born with different physical characteristics, they also come to us with differing emotional response styles. Some are shy around strangers, while others are quite gregarious. Some have a generally sunny disposition, while others seem perpetually sullen or gloomy. These inborn response styles are known as *temperament*, a concept of critical importance to parents who hope to stay connected with their children.

Temperament	**Inborn response style,**
+	
Experience	**family, friends, school, life…**
=	
Personality	**the "you" that people know.**

Temperament is not the same as *personality*, which is more of an end result—the character style that develops as a result of temperament and experience. While a child's temperament doesn't determine what kind of personality he or she will develop, it is the basic foundation upon which their character is built. A shy child can certainly become a brilliant performer or an effective CEO, but only if his sense of inner control and self-worth is strong. Parents can, of course, foster or hinder that inner strength, and much of that difference is determined by how they respond to their children's inborn temperament. Remember the way of the gardener—understand your child and encourage his natural path.

One of the best books for parents on this topic is Stanley Turecki's <u>The Difficult Child</u> (2000). In it he describes ten distinct temperamental traits. Each one is a continuum, and every child has his own pattern of highs and lows across the ten traits. Any particular pattern might be quite difficult for one parent to handle, while another parent might find it quite manageable. You know, one person's *overbearing* is another person's *enthusiastic*.

TEMPERAMENTAL TRAITS

Trait	Easier to Manage	More Challenging
Activity Level	Low to moderate	High, "hyperactive"
Self-control	Stronger, patient	Weaker, impulsive
Concentration	Stronger, stays with task	Weaker, distractible
Intensity	Low, mild, low-keyed	High, loud, forceful
Regularity	Regular, predictable	Irregular, spontaneous
Negative Persistence	Low, easily diverted	Won't give up easily
Sensory Threshold	High, unbothered	Low, physically sensitive
Initial Response	Approach, goes forward	Withdrawal, holds back
Adaptability	Stronger, flexible	Weaker, less flexible
Predominant Mood	Upbeat, cheerful	Subdued, serious

Adapted from Turecki, p.11 (2000)

Take a moment to review the various traits in the table above. Which aspects of your child's temperament are most challenging for you? Which of your own are challenging for others?

Extremes in temperamental traits, such as negative mood or stubbornness, can be annoying and inconvenient to be around. It's easy for the parent of such a child to frequently criticize and correct, a certain path to disconnection. When a child is repeatedly criticized for something that he feels he can't control, his self-worth suffers. When you understand your child's temperament, it should be easier for you to stop blaming him for this response style that he hasn't chosen.

THINK IT OVER, WRITE IT DOWN...

The most challenging aspect of my child's temperament is:

_____

_____

I can be more tolerant of the inconvenience by...

_____

_____.

It is your child's job in life to find a way to effectively meet his basic needs, given his unique temperament. It is your job as a parent to understand and work with your child's unique endowment—not to try to change it to a style that might be more comfortable for you.

What About ADHD?

This has become such a common diagnosis that it bears special mention. Attention Deficit Hyperactivity Disorder (ADHD) is not an illness. It is a description of a cluster of cognitive abilities that are weaker than those of most children. These mental skills are sometimes referred to as *executive functions,* because they carry out the quality control of our behavior. The cluster includes most importantly the functions of inhibition, concentration, organization, and planning. Kids who are described as ADHD (or ADD, without the physical hyperactivity) often have difficulty performing well in a conventional classroom. The demands for sitting still, sustained attention on low-interest tasks, and self-generated problem-solving are a poor match for the way these children's brains are wired. Parents often seek adjustments to classroom procedures to accommodate their children's differences. Some children with ADHD are placed in special education programs or alternative schools that are more experienced with this kind of student. Medication may even be prescribed to boost the child's ability to focus and inhibit disruptive responses.

I've seen each of these interventions work well for children, and I've seen each work poorly. To me the critical variables to be concerned about are,

1) How positively does the child regard himself despite his difference?
and, 2) How responsible does the child feel for completing quality work?

The two usually go hand-in-hand. Positive self-worth is tied to the basic need for power and is derived from accomplishing quality work. Again, your job as the parent of a child who has a difficult temperament is to carefully balance accommodation and expectation of responsibility for age-appropriate tasks. For example, your child should not be excused from homework but may need quite a bit of your involvement to stay focused and organized. Educate yourself; there are some good books about learning differences and ADHD that don't go overboard on the "disease model" (see recommended reading in the bibliography).

A Major Consequence

Another thing that makes staying connected difficult is your belief that as a responsible parent, you ought to be delivering consequences. Your child has just behaved badly, such as spilling juice all over the couch, or lying about having no homework yesterday, or taking the family car out without your permission. Shouldn't there be a consequence? Shouldn't you do something major? Absolutely. And here's the major consequence that I suggest: You and your child need to have a conversation about the problem. You can talk <u>with</u> your child about the problem, not <u>at</u> him or <u>for</u> him. Now I'm not saying that there shouldn't be other consequences, we'll get to that later. Please, trust me on this; if you're able to successfully engage your child in a conversation in which you stay connected and in which you appreciate his attempt to meet basic needs, you will have accomplished something very important. You'll have increased the chance that your child will consider his relationship with you, at least a bit, when he makes difficult behavior choices in the future. That's powerful stuff.

Consider this exchange between a working mom and her 13-year-old daughter:

Mom: *"Anna, we need to talk about the Internet."*
Anna: *"I can't believe you're after me about that again. Do you ever stop?"*
Mom: *"Do I ever stop? You're the one who never keeps her word. Just once I'd like to see you make an agreement that you live up to!"*
Anna: *"Right mom, are we done? I've got things to do."*

That really didn't go so well. Mom's opening was fine but as soon as she took a hit from Anna, she did what most people are inclined to do—she pushed back, and the connection was lost. This time, mom tries a new tool:

Mom: *"Anna, we need to talk about the Internet."*
Anna: *"I can't believe you're after me about that again. Do you ever stop?"*
Mom: *"I thought we had an agreement."*
Anna: *"Oh, come on. I just went on for a few minutes. I can't always wait for you to come home—my friends are online, and it's important that I hear what's going on."*
Mom: *"I know your friends are important."*
Anna: *"I don't think you do! You're trying to keep me out of the group. Right after school is when everyone's on!"*
Mom: *"I see what you mean. This is a tough problem."*
Anna: *"Well, I'm glad you're beginning to understand. Can't we do something about this ridiculous supervision rule?"*

Rather than pushing back, mom tried hard to stay connected. She never endorsed Anna's choice, but she did appreciate her desire to satisfy the belonging need. The Internet issue is not settled, but the stage is set for a cooperative effort to solve this tricky problem.

TIPS FOR STAYING CONNECTED

- *Avoid the 3 C's! Resist the urge to push back—Reach out instead.*

- *Listen for the <u>sense</u> of your child's behavior—his best attempt to satisfy a need (power, love, freedom, fun).*

- *Respect your child's temperament—don't try to change who he is.*

- *Believe that a connected conversation <u>is</u> an effective consequence.*

Sometimes just a connected conversation or two is enough to produce behavior change. Your child knows what you want and, as the relationship improves, his need for belonging will influence his choice of behaviors. If he persists in choosing problem behaviors, you can proceed to some of the more intensive tools that follow.

9. ENCOURAGE SELF-EVALUATION

Once you're speaking with your child about problems in a connected way, it will be possible to add more direction to the conversation. With the next tool, you'll encourage your child to evaluate her own behavior. This is an essential skill that we all want our children to develop.

The idea is really quite simple. Ask your child what she thinks about the quality of her effort. Now if you've not done much of this in the past, it will take a few episodes before you get much of an answer. Your child may feel as

> ## THE NEW TOOLS
>
> *1. Stay Connected*
>
> **2. Encourage Self-Evaluation**
>
> *3. Set Your Limits*
>
> *4. Plan Together*
>
> *5. Put Specials On Hold*

though she's being set up for a criticism, perhaps with good reason. The idea here is not to let her know what <u>you</u> think about the quality of her effort, but to encourage her to ask herself.

> Mom: *"How's that essay coming along?"*
> Daughter: *"I don't know. O.K. I guess."*
> Mom: *"Do you think you're doing a good job?"*
> Daughter (a bit annoyed): *"I know, you think I waited 'til the last minute, right?"*
> Mom: *"Oh, I don't really know. Do you have enough time to do well?"*
> Daughter (a bit puzzled): *"I think so. Yeah, it's going fine!"*

It will take some practice to inhibit your own impulse to criticize, especially when you have a strong view on the matter. Evaluate your own effort along the way. Remember what you want, and what you want most. Sure, you want her to do well on her essay, but what you want most is for her to take responsibility for her own happiness, success and well-being. Encouraging self-evaluation is the key to her making high-quality decisions in the future.

The best application for *self-evaluation* is when your child asks for help in solving a problem of her own. Many times the request is disguised as a helpless distress signal:

> *"I have absolutely no idea what I'm supposed to do for this English essay."*

She may feel a bit panicky because she can't readily find behavior to satisfy her need for power and achievement. The best effort she can come up with at the time may be to pressure you to solve her problem. Many parent-child conflicts take this form; the child is tantrumming about her inability to perform some required task and demanding that her parent relieve her burden. With *stay connected*, you can get through the encounter without increasing the conflict between you. With *self-evaluation*, you're going to try to do more. You're going to encourage your daughter to turn her attention inward and generate effective, quality behavior. In order to do this, you've got to firmly sustain the belief that…

…your child has the capability to generate effective, quality behavior.

This is the key. If you firmly maintain this belief, you'll convey the idea to your child. If you're well connected, your child will gradually come to believe you.

Daughter:	*"I have absolutely no idea what I'm supposed to do for this English essay. I can't come up with anything. You've got to give me some ideas!"*
Mom:	*"Sure, I'm happy to help. Tell me what ideas you've come up with so far?"*
Daughter:	*"Are you deaf? I told you I couldn't come up with anything!"*
Mom:	*"I see. Well, we'll need some kind of starting point—even an idea that you don't think would be the best."*
Daughter:	*"O.K., I thought of writing about my basketball team, but that's so lame."*
Mom:	*"I'm not sure I understand what's lame about that. I know you had a great time with your team."*
Daughter:	*"It's supposed to be about something I did that made a difference. I don't exactly think that basketball will save the world."*
Mom:	*"I see what you mean. Still, I'm sure you had something in mind when you thought about it, didn't you?"*
Daughter:	*"Well, I was thinking about how I helped that slow girl, Jessica—how I helped her get along better with the girls. But I think that's pretty lame, don't you?"*
Mom:	*"Not really. What's lame about it?"*
Daughter:	*"I don't think that just helping somebody out is what Mrs. Frazer means by making a difference."*
Mom:	*"Well, we don't know exactly what Mrs. Frazer would think, but do you think it made a difference?"*
Daughter:	*"It did to Jessica, I know that."*

Mom:	*"Do you think this is a topic you could do a good job with?"*
Daughter:	*"I'm not sure. I think so. Do you?"*
Mom:	*"I think so too. When you said it made a difference to Jessica, I think you said it all."*

Perhaps that encounter went a little too smoothly to be real, but it's best to learn from examples of success. The mom stayed connected and maintained her belief that the solution could come from her daughter. Mom did eventually provide her own opinion about her daughter's choice, but not until her daughter had self-evaluated. In reality, her daughter might have been more resistant—might have really punished her mother hard for being so useless with her help. In such a case, it's best to just say something like…

> *"Well, I'm trying the best that I can. Let's take a break and try again a bit later."*

Robert Wubbolding is a master trainer of choice psychology, and he has developed a counseling procedure that emphasizes the principle of self-evaluation. His method centers around four questions that serve as an excellent orienting device for anyone who is trying to help someone solve a problem. Dr. Wubbolding says, "Tune in to radio W D E P."

> **W—What is it that you really want?**
> **D—What are you currently doing?**
> **E—How well is it working (evaluation)?**
> **P—Can you try something different (plan)?**

Keep these questions in mind while you're talking with your child. Try hard not to take the bait, not to accept the idea that your child can't solve his problem. If he comes up with a plan that you think is pretty shaky, ask if <u>he</u> thinks that it will do the job. If he sticks with it, you should try hard to stick with it, too. Remember, today you want him to get along better with his gym teacher, but what you want most is for him to self-evaluate and generate creative solutions.

Here are some questions that encourage self-evaluation:

> *What have you tried so far?*
> *How well did that work out?*
> *Can you think of anything else that might help?*
> *If it was going really well, what would that look like?*

Are you satisfied with the effort you put in?
Is it enough to do the job?
Remember the problem we were talking about yesterday—How did your plan work out?

TIPS FOR ENCOURAGING SELF-EVALUATION

- *Resist the urge to offer your solution.*
- *Listen for some creative behavior your child has tried or is thinking about trying.*
- *Ask him to evaluate his own effectiveness.*
- *Resist the urge to correct your child's self-evaluation!*

10. SET YOUR LIMITS

With so much emphasis on eliminating external control, you might get the impression that choice parenting means parenting without limits. This is certainly not the case. In order to learn to effectively meet their basic needs, children require clear and predictable guidelines. That's really what limit setting ought to be about—providing good information about the boundaries of acceptable behavior. The limits that are being set are the "tipping points," the levels and sorts of behavior that will result in strong responses from parents, teachers, friends, and neighbors. It's essential information, and without it children will be unable to find happiness and satisfaction.

> ## THE NEW TOOLS
>
> *1. Stay Connected*
>
> *2. Encourage Self-Evaluation*
>
> *3. Set Your Limits*
>
> *4. Plan Together*
>
> *5. Put Specials On Hold*

When children test limits and ask for more than we've offered, they're displaying their need for freedom. They want to feel as though they're choosing their own path, not being controlled by others. Too much freedom, however, will feel unsafe and overwhelming. It's our job as parents to be attuned to how much freedom our children can reasonably handle at any given point in their development, and to adjust our limits accordingly.

Remember the conversation between the mom and her six-year-old who wanted another cookie (Chapter 4)? In that case of effective limit setting, the mom let her daughter know quite clearly what the limit was, without demanding to control her daughter's behavior. She gave the information and let her daughter make her choice. It's really all we can ever do.

Unfortunately, some people's idea of limit setting is continually dictating to their children what they must always and must never do.

> *"You must do your homework!"*
> *"Don't you dare hit your brother!"*
> *"You have to pick up your room!"*
> *"Don't even think about going to see that movie!"*

If this sounds like you, you must be exhausted. It's a lot of work being an external control parent. The tone is all wrong, too, because it violates the first element of choice psychology—*internal control.* Because all we can really control is our own behavior, telling our kids what they must and mustn't do is fraught with problems. Of course they know what you really mean when you say,

"Now listen up—you'd better be home by 10:00, or else!"

It means that you'll be really angry, and might punish them if they come home late. And you better deliver, too, because when you threaten to punish and don't follow through, you send an important message. You child learns that defying your orders may well be worth the risk.

Here's how to avoid this mess. Put the emphasis on <u>your</u> behavior, not your child's. It's why I call it *Setting <u>Your</u> Limits.* Rather than telling your child what he must do, tell him what you want. Rather than telling him what he cannot do, tell him what kind of thing is really upsetting to you. You're telling him about your limits—about your picture of reasonable behavior. You're depending on the strength of your relationship to influence his choice.

"I'd like you to be home by 10:00."

Is this just a difference in words? Well it could be, but I'm suggesting something a lot more than new words. I'm suggesting that you convey to your child, as you establish limits, that you fully understand that he'll choose his own behavior. Don't let the allure of pushing your weight around divert you from the essence of this important task. You're giving your child information, telling him the limits of behavior that are acceptable to you. To the extent that you can restrain yourself from using the hammer, your child can't help but feel responsible for his own choice. That's what you want most.

Dad:	*"I'd like you to be home by 10:00 tonight."*
Son:	*"Oh come on, you've got to be kidding! The game will just be getting over then."*
Dad:	*"I know you want some time with your friends, but it's a school night, and 10:00 is as late as I'm comfortable with."*
Son:	*"How about 11:00? All my homework is finished."*
Dad:	*"No, 10:00 is when I'd like you to be home."*
Son:	*"Whatever."*

Maybe he will, and maybe he won't. But he always had that choice, didn't he? Remember, if he defies your limit you'll have new information, and new choices, to consider. A good idea might be to have a very connected conversation about his behavior—a conversation in which you'll encourage him to self-evaluate.

There are times when simply setting your limits won't do, and it's more appropriate to exert real external control. This is the case when physical safety is an issue. There's no point in allowing a twelve year old to continue hitting his younger brother while you patiently let him know that it's not the choice you would prefer. It's always important to be clear that safety comes first and, as a parent, you are willing to use whatever power you need to protect the safety of your child and others. Similarly, with younger children (under the age of five, or so) it's sometimes necessary to physically redirect them, using your own power to limit their choices in a safer direction. (I remember clearly the time my father yanked me across the kitchen, as I playfully poked at the electrical outlet with a piece of picture hanging wire.) Be mindful that control always costs some degree of connection, so use it sparingly. As you use more choice psychology in your life, you're likely to find that the occasions when power is necessary are surprisingly rare. William Glasser once explained that parenting with choice theory is really preventive—if it is used early on, the kind of discipline problems that require external control are seldom seen.

Here's a very common scenario with a younger child:

> *Mom:* "I don't want you to sit in front of the TV all morning. Don't you think that it's been about enough?"
>
> *Child:* "Oh come on—it's O.K. Besides, this is my favorite show."
>
> *Mom:* "I really mean it. An hour and a half is enough for today. I'd like you to find some other things to do."
>
> *Child:* "Mom, please! I have to watch this show."
>
> *Mom:* "It does look pretty good. When are you willing to turn the TV off?"
>
> *Child:* "Right after this show, O.K?"
>
> *Mom:* "Well, I guess that would be O.K. with me. Let's talk later about setting up some rules about this."
>
> *Child:* "O.K., sure."

This kind of clear message, coupled with a willingness to compromise, is a recipe for effective limit setting. It's so much more successful than the "*do it now—because I said so,*" approach. When you avoid the temptation to overpower your child, and you try hard to stay connected, you can usually reach an acceptable agreement. The more you do this at early ages, the easier it will be later when the stakes are higher.

TIPS FOR SETTING YOUR LIMITS

- *Be clear about what you want.*
- *Try not to devalue the behavior you're hoping to limit.*
- *Keep the focus on <u>your</u> wants, rather than what your child <u>must</u> do.*
- *Avoid overpowering—be willing to compromise.*

11. PLAN TOGETHER

Mom:	*"O.K., let's talk about that T.V. situation."*
Child:	*"Do we have to now? I'm kind of busy."*
Mom:	*"Well, I would like to work out some new rules. I thought we had an agreement before, but it really isn't working too well."*
Child:	*"Yeah, O.K. So, what do you want?"*

> **THE NEW TOOLS**
>
> *1. Stay Connected*
>
> *2. Encourage Self-Evaluation*
>
> *3. Set Your Limits*
>
> *4. Plan Together*
>
> *5. Put Specials On Hold*

Planning together is a good technique to use with behavior problems that continue over time. Remember, your child's persistently disruptive or self-defeating behavior is his current best attempt to meet some basic need. He's using the best plan currently at his disposal. Your job is to let him know that his plan isn't working for you, and that a new one is needed.

You don't want to just demand that he stop doing whatever he's doing; better to help him find a more effective way to meet his needs. A son may curse frequently at the dinner table, trying to feel powerful and important. A daughter may routinely lie about homework assignments, trying to preserve more time for fun. In both cases, the children compromise satisfying relationships with their parents in order to meet other needs. If they could find effective ways to satisfy both, they would.

So many parents tell me that their children with such miserable behavior at home are regarded as very well mannered by the rest of the world. These kids haven't found a way to effectively balance their competing needs, so of course they choose to compromise family relationships. They can afford to—it's unlikely that they'll be thrown out. If you let your child know that the current plan isn't acceptable to you, your child will respond in one of three ways: He'll ignore you, he'll argue with you, or he'll plan with you.

- If he ignores you, **be persistent.** Don't overpower or insist on a conversation, but let him know by coming back to the issue that you really mean it—you want to discuss it. *"When would be a good time?"*

- If he argues with you, **stay connected.** Make it clear that you don't want to fight—and don't! *"I'm trying hard not to fight with you. Maybe we should try again to talk about this later."*
- If he agrees to have a **planning conversation** with you, then you're off and running.

Ingredients of a good plan:

- **Simple:** It should be uncomplicated—something you can describe in one brief sentence.
- **Observable:** Anyone can see if the plan is being carried out; it states what will be done, rather than what won't.
- **Realistic:** It is well within the child's grasp to carry out this plan.
- **Mutual:** The more the child has input, the better the plan. A straight suggestion from an adult is a weak plan.
- **Controlled by the child:** It's something the child can carry out regardless of external circumstances. It's not conditional, not a "quid pro quo."
- **Committed:** It's best to get a firm commitment to carry out the plan. "Yes, I will" is far superior to, "Well, I'll try."

A few good plans that include those ingredients:

- I'll put my clothes out the night before.
- I'll call home by 3:30 and let you know what I'm doing.
- I'll walk away when I feel like cursing at him.

A few plans that are not so good, because they lack an important ingredient:

- I'll think hard about treating my brother better. (not observable)

- I'll <u>try</u> to come home on time. (no commitment)
- I'll do all of my homework, if you stop spying on me. (conditional, not entirely in child's control)
- I'll set my alarm for 7:00, and if I'm not up by 7:15, you wake me twice, except on days when I have band, then you wake me at 6:45. (what do you think?)

Now, let's get back to the television conversation:

Mom: *"I think there should be some limit on how much T.V. you're watching. Don't you?"*

Child: *"I don't know. As long as my homework is done, what's the difference?"*

Mom: *"Well, I've noticed that when you watch for a long time, you get lazy and not interested in talking or doing other things. I'm the same way. I really think there should be some limit."*

Child: *"O.K. I'll try not to watch as much."*

Mom: *"Well, that's fine, but it's not really enough for me. We've had this T.V. conversation before, and this time I think we need a more specific plan.*

Child: *"I don't know what you mean."*

Mom: *"I'm sure we can come up with something that we can both live with."*

Child: *"Oh, come on, you mean like time limits?"*

Mom: *"Well, that's one idea. What's so bad about that?"*

Child: *"I'll tell you what's bad about it. What if there's something really great on, and I've already used my limit? I don't want to be tied down to some stupid number."*

Mom: *"Well, we could try time limits, and allow occasional exceptions when there's something really great on. What kind of time limit seems fair to you?"*

Child: *"O.K. How about, one hour after homework is done, and no limits on the weekend."*

Mom: *"I can live with the first part, but I really would like some limit on the weekends, too. How about one hour during the day, and no limit after dinner?"*

Child: *"Yeah, that sounds good. If we start now, I get a fresh hour, right?"*

Mom: *"Sure, why not. You know, you'll make a great lawyer one day."*

This plan has a good chance of success because it's simple, specific, and the child was involved in its creation. Even though all of the essential ingredients were met, it could still fall apart. The child could forget, or more likely, test his mother to see what <u>her</u> level of commitment is. It's always a good idea to have a "self-evaluation" conversation some time after a new plan has been implemented. It's an opportunity to remind the child of the agreement and to further demonstrate that you're not trying to control him.

Mom:	*(Two days later) "How's the new T.V. plan going? Are you following it?"*
Child:	*"Yeah, I'm following it. It's really not so bad, and I get to watch enough. I'm worried about the MTV awards next week, though."*
Mom:	*"Really, what's the problem?"*
Child:	*"Well I'm only supposed to watch one hour on weeknights, but I really want to watch that whole show—and it's going to be long."*
Mom:	*"True, but I think our plan allows for special exceptions. Do you think this qualifies?"*
Child:	*"Most definitely!"*
Mom:	*"O.K., fine. How late do you think it makes sense to stay up?"*
Child:	*"Well, I really want to stay up for the whole thing. I'm not going to kid you; it may run 'til midnight. But I'll do all my work first, O.K.?"*
Mom:	*"If you think you can get yourself to school on time the next day, I'll go along with it."*
Child:	*"Excellent!"*

This mom is really doing well. She understands that she's getting quite a bit of what she wants, namely that her son is in the planning conversation! It's a good idea to be generous and flexible when you're planning together. Remember what you want, and what you want <u>most</u>. You may want compliance, but more than that you want your child to develop a sense of inner control and responsibility. He may or may not follow through on the T.V. agreement. The important thing is that he's in the conversation, planning in a responsible way about limits and choices. As he learns that he can effectively meet his needs by planning cooperatively with others, he'll be more likely to choose this course in the future. If he continues to break the agreements, there's still another level of technique that you can step up to. In most cases though, you won't have to.

A Planning Conversation

By the way, *planning together* is also a great preventive tool. When you're about to embark on an activity or event that carries some risk for unhappiness or conflict, you can use planning to head off the trouble. It's different from what we've been discussing because you're not asking for a change; instead you're asking your child to think about how he plans to meet his needs. I always like to have a planning conversation in the car when we're on our way to some family activity, be it a vacation or just out to dinner. The idea is to allow everyone to clarify their wants, and in this way to assume some responsibility for their own satisfaction and happiness.

Here's an example of some planning before visiting grandparents in Florida:

Dad:	*"Before we all get on the plane, why don't we each say what we're hoping for on this trip? I'll start: I'm hoping to get out on the tennis court two or three times during the week. That shouldn't be a problem, cause I'll play early."*
Mom:	*"I'd rather you didn't play tomorrow though; Let's settle in first before you run off."*
Dad:	*"That's fine."*
Younger son:	*"I want to drive Grandpa's golf cart a lot, even more than last year. Can I?"*
Dad:	*"I think so, but let's be sure Grandpa's O.K. with it. You know, he likes to be asked. It's never been a problem before, so I'm sure it'll be O.K".*
Older son:	*"There's really nothing I feel like doing. I still can't believe I have to spend the whole vacation week away. This sucks."*
Mom:	*"I know it's not your favorite way to spend your week off, but you might as well make the best of it. Isn't there anything you'd like to do while we're down there?"*
Older son:	*"Not a thing."*
Mom:	*"Well, if you do think of something, let us know. We'll do our best to help you make it happen."*

Even the older son named a want, although his was quite unrealistic. He preferred not to be on the trip in the first place. Nonetheless, he was given the opportunity to make his position clear, and it was accepted without much criticism. That can never hurt the connection between them. Mom's elegant response conveyed that she was available to help, and also that it was the boy's responsibility to clarify his wants. She found a much better position to be in than to knock herself out trying to please a sullen teenager.

THINK IT OVER, WRITE IT DOWN...

Think of an ongoing problem in your household that could use a new plan. How might you begin the conversation?

_____

_____

_____

_____.

12. PUT SPECIALS ON HOLD

CAUTION! This tool should be used sparingly; it does contain external control. Please understand that if you faithfully apply the first four tools, you'll rarely need to use *specials on hold.* But there is a time when pure parental power is needed to interrupt problem behavior. When have you reached that point? It's certainly time for external control when aggressive or dangerous behavior has become common. A child who is frequently hitting people, breaking things, using drugs, or stealing has more freedom than he can safely handle. One mother consulted me about her ten-year-old son's violent tirades and

> ## THE NEW TOOLS
>
> *1. Stay Connected*
>
> *2. Encourage Self-Evaluation*
>
> *3. Set Your Limits*
>
> *4. Plan Together*
>
> *5. Put Specials On Hold*

confessed that she often locked herself in the family car, seeking refuge in the driveway. It was definitely time for external control. It also makes sense to consider this tool when your child is stuck in a long period of self-defeating behavior. A young child who loses a backpack every other day, or an older child who repeatedly oversleeps and misses his first period class, might each respond to *putting specials on hold.* Remember, this tool should only be used after you've put a solid effort into setting your limits and planning together.

Simply put, here's the idea: If your child persists in some problematic behavior despite repeated efforts to plan together, you should reduce his freedom. It's best to remove some goodies or privileges that are related to the problem behavior. They're not gone forever, or even for a specific time period. They're on hold—like money placed in escrow. Don't worry; I haven't abandoned my fundamental convictions about control and connection. There is a way to do this without weakening the relationship with your child. It's tricky, but if you've learned steps one through four, you can handle this one, too.

Specials on Hold closely resembles the behavioral intervention known as *Response Cost.* That is the removal of something of value, following a behavior that you hope to eliminate. Do you remember the Soup Nazi on *Seinfeld?* He was a master of this technique; *"No soup for you!"* Because it is imposed externally, to discourage behavior, response cost is a form of punishment. *Specials on Hold* differs from response cost and all punishments in one very important respect: The child retains a high degree of control over the return of the lost privilege.

Instead of,

> *"You're grounded for a month!"*

Or even,

> *"You're grounded until further notice"!*

We're going to try,

> *"You're staying in for a while. I don't really know for how long, but certainly until we have a curfew plan that we can agree on."*

PUNISHMENT	SPECIALS ON HOLD
Often imposed suddenly, in an emotional context.	*Always used after good faith attempts to plan together.*
Time limits are fixed, or unspecified.	*Sanctions end when effective planning begins.*
Intention is to exact a cost on the child.	*Intention is to renew efforts to plan together.*

Here's an example of specials on hold with a six-year-old boy. He's been throwing things around in his room when frustrated or unhappy, and recently broke a lamp in the process. His Dad has had several talks with him, but despite promises to do better, the behavior has persisted.

> David: "Hey, where's all my stuff?"
>
> Dad: "Well, we've decided to put some things away for a while."
>
> David: "You mean my Game Boy, my Pokeymon cards? Hey, where's all my stuffed animals?"
>
> Dad: "You know, I really meant it when I said that throwing things around in your room was a problem. We're holding onto your stuff because you're not really taking good care of things."
>
> David: "What? That's not fair! (Crying,) I need my animals!"
>
> Dad: "I know you do, and I'm sure that you'll have them back soon. But we've got to find a better way to protect these things. I'm concerned that they're not safe."
>
> David: (screaming)"Give me my animals back!"
>
> Dad: "I want you to have all of your things back. We need to talk about it though. I'll come back a little later, when you're less upset."

After a surprisingly brief period of hysteria, David asks his Dad to come talk with him about his animals. The possibility for planning together has been established.

David: "O.K. Dad. I promise not to throw anything in my room any-more. Can I have my stuff back?"

Dad: "I'm glad that you want to work this out with me. Now what's going to be different this time? I think you promised before—we've got to come up with something new, don't you think?"

David: "What do you mean? I said I won't throw anything!"

Dad: "I need to hear what you'll do differently when you're upset. Any ideas?"

David: "Well, I could yell and scream—that won't hurt anything."

Dad: "Yeah, that's not a bad idea. If it goes on for too long though, it's pretty upsetting for the rest of the family. Would screaming for one or two minutes be enough to help you feel better?"

David: "Yeah. I'll only scream for one or two minutes. Can I have my stuff back?"

Dad: "Sure, let's give this plan a try."

Again, a self-evaluation conversation should follow before too much time has passed. The dad might ask,

"How's the new plan going? Are you keeping all your stuff safe and well pro-tected?"

Putting specials on hold is really a form of limit setting. You're clearly telling your child what you want—a new plan for some problem behavior. Instead of using threats to demand that planning take place, you remove a set of privileges or spe-cial treats. The proper tone is essential, because you're trying to encourage con-nection in the form of collaborative planning. If you threaten or blame, you make it very difficult for your child to join you in a cooperative effort. If you're too angry to do this without hostility, then you need to take a walk, and come back to this tool later.

Remember Steve, the divorced parent with custody of his ten-year-old son, Jackie? The boy was in deep trouble with schoolteachers because of his disre-spect and disruptiveness in class. Steve had been punishing and yelling, and had most recently taken his son's beloved Game Boy away.

Steve agreed to try a new approach, but it was very important to him not to give the Game Boy back too easily. "He's got to learn to be responsible about school," Steve explained. "He can't just show up, do no work, and be rude. There's got to be a consequence!" Steve was willing to stop yelling at Jackie, if I could help him find a more effective way to deal with the school behavior problems. I told him about the "specials on hold" technique.

For Steve, the plan was to tell his son that the Game Boy, computer, and Play Station were all being placed "on hold." Clearly, school wasn't working out well for Jackie, and they needed to put all their attention into a new plan that would lead to a better experience there. The key to the success of this plan was for Steve to convey to his son that he truly <u>wanted</u> him to have his stuff back, and that he could certainly have it back just as soon a new plan for school success was in place.

Jackie: (pretty angry)"This is crazy! It's not my fault that the teachers in that stupid school are so uptight. You have to give me my stuff back."
Steve: (fairly calm) "I know how much you enjoy your games, and I want you to have them as soon as possible. But school is really important, and you've got to take care of your work before you can play."
Jackie: "This is the wackiest thing you've ever done. You think stealing my stuff is going to make me listen to my teachers?" (screaming and crying, now) "You better give it back or you'll have some fight on your hands!"
Steve: "Look, I'm trying real hard not to fight with you. Maybe now is not the best time to talk about it, but when you're ready, I'll be happy to help you put a new plan together."

Jackie basically shut his Dad out for two days, after which he asked for his stuff back saying that, after all, he'd "been good."

Steve: *"I really meant it. Let's work out a school plan first."*
Jackie: *"Dad, you don't understand. I can't do well in this school—it's so different from my old school, and I don't understand a lot of the work."*
Steve: *"I wondered if the work was too difficult, but your teacher assured me that when you're paying attention, you always know what you're doing."*
Jackie: *"Maybe I only pay attention when I know what they're doing!"*

Steve: "O.K. It sounds like you may need some extra help. Should we get a tutor?"

Jackie: "No way! I'm not giving up more of my free time for schoolwork. Besides, Jimmy Fox has a tutor, and she's crabby, and he hates her."

Steve: "Well, if I hire a tutor that you don't like, that would be a really bad plan, don't you think?"

Jackie: "Would I get to choose the tutor?"

Steve: "You can have veto power, if you give it a real chance. Would that help you get involved in school?"

Jackie: "Yes, definitely. I can really get rid of her if I don't like her?"

Steve: "Absolutely. And as long as you're trying hard, you can play your games again."

Obviously the key for Jackie was to feel some power and self-worth. When he realized that he had a say in the tutor selection, his motivation shifted.

Sure, you can choose to punish your child with a harsh sanction or an angry attitude, but what will that accomplish? A punishing approach will accomplish a few things:

1) You may feel in greater control of the situation than you were before—that's a plus;

2) Your child will learn to be more careful about getting caught—that's not bad, I guess;

3) Your child will be less inclined to create a new solution, will feel less connected with you, and will be less interested in following your suggestions—that is definitely not good.

Specials on hold, like all of the new tools described here, is a specific way of applying choice psychology to parent-child problems. There's nothing magical about this technique. In fact, unless it's delivered with the proper mindset, it won't be of much help. However, if you put the relationship first, and stay connected while you take this action, you're likely to get a very good result.

TIPS FOR SPECIALS ON HOLD

- *Wait until you're not being angry—give yourself a chance to do this well.*

- *Don't use this to coerce or punish—choose a more compassionate attitude.*

- *Try to be steadfast and calm about your intention to maintain the limits you've set.*

- *Convey a willing interest to take specials off hold when planning together is actually happening.*

SECTION THREE
RESPONDING TO DIFFICULT BEHAVIOR

These next several chapters use real people and real problems to illustrate the principles and tools of choice parenting. The examples come from my office practice and from parenting workshops that I conduct. Of course the names and some details have been altered to protect everyone's confidentiality, but the stories are quite accurate. In my practice, I sometimes work directly with a child, and sometimes with the parents only. In most cases I weave back and forth, helping parents find a more effective response to their children's behavior problems. The examples in these chapters represent the kinds of problems I encounter most frequently and my suggestions to the concerned parents who present them.

The kind of psychotherapy that I practice is called Reality Therapy, and it principally involves teaching people choice psychology and helping them to apply it to their lives. But formal psychotherapy is not the only way to improve your behavioral and emotional health. Anytime you use new information to help you choose better behavior, and change your experience to a more satisfying picture, I would consider that to be a form of therapy. Reading this book, taking a trip with your son through the Grand Canyon, starting a new diet and exercise program—any of these might prove to be your best therapy.

Do You Need Professional Help?

I began writing this book because I wanted to give my patients a companion resource for our work together. I soon realized that these principles and tools could stand on their own and be of help to parents, whether or not they'd decided to consult a psychologist. But how do you know when you should get professional help? Certainly, a professional should be consulted if dangerous behavior is present, such as self-harm or drug abuse. I would also say that if you or your child are unhappy for a sustained period, and despite your best efforts you can't find an effective way to improve matters, it's a good idea to get outside help. Don't be fooled into thinking that sustained unhappiness is "normal" for this or that stage of development. No one keeps his or her balance at all times, but the normal state of affairs for anyone is to be relatively happy and productive.

Here is a good basic assessment of your child's emotional functioning:

> *Think of the four basic needs, and ask yourself these questions:*
>
> - *Can my child find effective ways to experience success, in and out of school (power, achievement and self-worth)?*
> - *Does my child enjoy his relationships with family and friends (love and belonging)?*
> - *Does my child generate ideas about what he wants and what he'd like to do (freedom)?*
> - *Is my child able to play and enjoy learning about new things (fun)?*

You probably have concerns about one or more of these areas, and that's the reason you're reading this book. I believe that the use of choice psychology in parenting can help to improve nearly all child behavior problems. I'm certain that it can't hurt. But these kinds of problems and conflicts are emotionally charged, and not all parents can maintain their objectivity and commitment without some outside help. My suggestion is to do what makes sense to you. Don't hesitate to see a specialist if you think it will help you. And don't rush your child into therapy because somebody told you he needs it. You're in charge—do what makes good sense to you. If, after a reasonable effort, things are not improving, it's time to do something different.

13. WHY IS HE DOING THIS? The Meaning of Problem Behavior

Choice psychology provides part of the answer to why your child is being so difficult. He's making the best attempt available to him to satisfy basic needs for power, belonging, freedom and fun—needs that are common to us all. It's not easy for him to accomplish this balancing act; that's what he's trying to gain a sense of control over. He's not trying to make your life miserable, or his for that matter. If he could come up with a less troublesome way to meet his various needs, he would. The child who is exhibiting serious behavior problems—problems that interfere with basic areas of function such as school, friendships, and family life—is an unhappy child. He has not yet found an effective way to match his inner pictures with the outer world. As long as his wants are unfulfilled, he'll generate all sorts of behavior (action, thinking, emotion, physiology) in a persistent attempt to regain emotional balance and a sense of inner control.

> *Your child is always trying to maintain a sense of balance and inner control.*

But <u>why</u> is he having so much difficulty? Parents invariably want to know what is causing the problem.

> *Is it genetic? Are we bad parents? Why is <u>our</u> child so defiant (or depressed, or inattentive)?*

The more traditional mental health approaches concentrate on "causal explanations." They point to early childhood events, intergenerational family patterns, or neuro-biological brain chemistry to answer the "why" question. Many parents welcome causal explanations, hoping to increase their sense of inner control in the face of a very frustrating experience. Sometimes the explanation offered is in the form of a diagnosis, which really isn't an explanation at all. Consider the experience of a very nice couple that I recently met with:

> *The Stanleys went to a prestigious child study group to find out what was wrong with Terrance, their perpetually angry six-year-old. Mrs. Stanley gave a detailed report to the evaluator, describing her son's negative and angry attitude, his frequent resistance to their direction, and his extreme hostility and defiance to their authority. Terrance was then thoroughly tested and interviewed. Some time later the Stanleys met with the coordinator of the team, who informed them that their child had ODD, Oppositional Defiant Disorder.*

> *"At last," Mrs. Stanley thought. "We've finally found the person who will tell us why our son is behaving this way." She eagerly asked the doctor what this Oppositional Defiant Disorder was—what did it mean? In turn, he carefully explained to her that, with ODD, they could expect Terrance to exhibit a pattern of negativistic, hostile and defiant behavior, frequently including arguments with adults, defiance of rules, and an angry mood. "Well of course," responded a disappointed Mr. Stanley. "That's what we told you!"*

A diagnosis is a highly reliable <u>description</u> of problem behavior, but it explains very little. It does have its uses, foremost among them is efficient communication among professionals. But how much value does a label add to your effort to help your child? Not too much, I'm afraid.

A Better Question

Part of the problem here is with the question itself. Asking, "Why?" tends to pull you in the direction of external control explanations. It leads to answers like...

> ...*she has a chemical imbalance,*
> ...*he has an attention deficit disorder,* or
> ...*she has low self-esteem.*

These explanations are constructed in terms that are largely out of your and your child's direct control. As such, they are most useful if you are considering external control remedies such as medication or behavior modification. While these interventions can sometimes be useful, they shouldn't be the first steps that you take to help your child.

A better question than W*hy?*, is *What?* Actually, a series of *what* questions is best of all. It's the same group of questions that make up the self-evaluation we spoke of earlier:

> ### THE BEST QUESTIONS OF ALL
>
> - *What does my child want most?*
> - *What is he doing to try to get it?*
> - *What could he do differently that might be more effective?*
> - *What can I do differently that might encourage him to try something new?*

I'm sure you can see that these *what* questions lead you to choices that are more in your direct control. You can't directly raise your child's esteem or change his history. You can't directly change his brain chemistry unless you administer drugs, and neither can he, but you can each choose new behavior that more effectively satisfies basic emotional needs. When you do, self-esteem and brain chemistry will come right along with it.

> *The Stanleys began to think about their child and their parenting from a choice psychology perspective. They realized that it wasn't easy for Terrance to effectively meet his needs for power and freedom. When given even a simple directive to stop playing video games and come to dinner, for example, he easily felt overpowered and anxious and worked hard to regain inner control by fighting, protesting, and demanding. His parents learned to give*

directions differently to him than they might to their other children. They gave him plenty of information, plenty of choice, and plenty of room. They had to learn to do a lot of things differently. In time, Terrance began to be more cooperative. Rather than digging in his heals and being obstinate, he learned that he could take his time and then join the family. In a few short months, the Oppositional Defiant Disorder disappeared.

Why Does He <u>Keep</u> Doing It?

Most of what we consider to be *problem behavior* is compulsive. This means that the child feels compelled to repeatedly engage in it, despite the fact that it is getting him into quite a bit of trouble. Why would a child continue to steal from his sister or lie about homework despite very unpleasant consequences? It is because the behavior he's choosing is <u>marginally</u> satisfying to him. In some way, it helps him satisfy a portion of his emotional need-set. It may muck up some other part of his life, like his relationship with his parents, but it is partially satisfying, and that may be the best that he can come up with right now. So he pushes on with the same unfortunate behavior.

> *Marginally satisfying behavior becomes compulsive if one lacks the awareness, confidence, or courage to try something different.*

It's much more difficult to change horses than to stay on the one you're currently riding, even if it's not taking you in the most desirable direction. To change behavior requires courage and creativity, and that only happens in a very supportive environment. A child who's been in trouble a lot feels judged and criticized and is unlikely to take the emotional risk of trying new behavior. If he's doing poorly in school for example, he feels off-balance and will generate some corrective behavior. If he's unsure how to bring his grades up, he may choose to lie to his parents about his homework, and that might actually produce a sense of inner power and control. When he is found out and gets into some sort of trouble, he may still find this imperfect solution to be worth it. Being deceptive is familiar to him and trying a new way of studying seems unknown and rather frightening. Lying is marginally satisfying, and he sticks with it. If he gets into more trouble, he just might push even harder rather than take the emotional risk of changing horses.

> **THINK IT OVER, WRITE IT DOWN...**
>
> A child is more likely to take creative chances in an atmosphere of emotional safety. What can I do to create that safety in my family?
>
> _____
>
> _____
>
> _____.

This idea of the marginally satisfying solution sheds some light on the familiar experience of the "terrible" child who is so well liked in all his friends' homes. It's difficult to balance many and various needs. This child may feel that he can afford to abuse his family members, as they are more likely to be forgiving. The fact that he shows restraint and social skill when dealing with his friends' parents is to his credit. At home he settles for a less complete solution—he's willing to trade some belonging for power and freedom.

And, of course, we've all heard this common explanation for a child's difficult behavior:

> *"Oh, he's just doing it for attention."*

This has always bothered me, not so much because of inaccuracy, but because it's so dismissive. It makes it seem unimportant that the child desperately wants someone to know that he has a problem. If a child is working that hard to get somebody's attention, you can be sure that there's an unmet need that's of utmost importance to him. Dismiss him, and you put your connection at risk.

Flexibility about Inner Pictures

For an unhappy child to regain a sense of inner control and emotional balance, he'll have to change some aspect of his behavior. That means changing his inner picture of what he wants or the ways he's willing to go about getting what he wants. Instead of seeing himself at the movies right now, for example, he might have to change his inner picture to being at the movies tomorrow afternoon. Some children are quite flexible and can change their pictures readily. Others are more rigid and have difficulty letting go of a picture once they have created it.

Obviously, the more flexible one has an advantage. Although this kind of adaptability was described earlier as a temperamental trait, I've found that people can learn to be more flexible—more able to change their inner pictures. This is why, when planning together with your child, you always encourage him to generate new and different ideas. You're teaching him to be flexible and to consider alternate ways to satisfy basic needs. By the way, parents also need flexibility to effectively connect with their children. Many of the suggestions in this book will require you to change your inner pictures of how you parent. Don't worry; grown-ups can also learn to be more flexible.

Emotional Reactivity

Another reason that your child persists in behaving badly has to do with how emotionally reactive you are to him. Consider the following question:

Does your child make you upset?

Of course the literal truth is that no, no one outside of you can *make* you upset. You generate your own total behavior, which includes upset feelings. But none of us want to be so disconnected from our children that their actions don't affect us. On the other hand, it's possible to be too connected, a condition called *fusion*. With this extreme level of reactivity, you feel as though your responses are controlled and determined by those of your child. Your basic need for freedom is seriously compromised. Fusion includes the belief, *"if my child is upset then I, too, must be upset."*

EMOTIONAL REACTIVITY

LOW   HIGH

———————————————————————————————————▶

Disconnection   Well-Balanced Connection   Fusion

If you're highly reactive and feeling little freedom, you're likely to choose an overpowering behavior rather than a connecting one. You may feel locked into a pattern of anger, resentment, and retribution or submission. Whenever you feel as though you have no choice about how you might respond, there's a good chance that you're emotionally fused. Don't worry, it's not a fatal condition—you just might need to practice responses that help you reduce your reactivity.

THINK IT OVER, WRITE IT DOWN...

In what situation are you inclined to become highly reactive?

_____

_____

_____.

What behavior/activity helps you reduce your reactivity?

1)_____

2)_____

3)_____

Personally, I've learned to give myself a little private choice psychology pep talk:

> *O.K. Rich, it feels as though he's controlling you right now, but you know that you can choose not to be so upset. Just try to let his barbs pass by. You don't have to fight back. Take a deep breath and try to stay calm.*

No kidding; this really works for me.

So how does emotional fusion contribute to your child's persistently difficult behavior? When you feel you are being controlled and retaliate in some way, your child may actually feel an increased sense of inner control and power. Remember, he's having trouble satisfying basic needs, and that produces an "out-of-control" feeling. When he manipulates or engages you in a reactive battle, even if he loses, he does marginally satisfy his need for power and control. He still knows how to "make you" upset, or perhaps how to "make you" give in.

Emotional Symptoms

Children express their unhappiness in many different ways. The total behaviors that they generate when their basic needs are frustrated are often referred to as symptoms. You'll recall that total behavior has four aspects—action, thought, feeling, and physiology. Consequently, the symptoms that children generate can take any of these forms.

There's an old saw among child therapists:

"Boys act out, and girls act in."

Of course it's a generalization, but there is some truth to it. Boys tend to generate more outer-directed or disruptive symptoms to express their unhappiness. They may *act* aggressively (pushing, hitting, throwing, using drugs), and *feel* anger and hostility (blame and upset directed at others).

Girls tend to generate more inner-directed symptoms to express their unhappiness. They may *act* withdrawn (shut down, get quiet, isolate), and *feel* depressed (self-blame, hopeless), and activate their *physiology* (headaches, g.i. problems).

You'll notice that I describe symptoms as behavior that we generate, rather than as maladies that befall us. Anxiety, depression, anger—these are all emotional expressions of total behavior. They are part of a discouraged person's generated response, his attempt to gain a sense of inner control when the world is disappointing him. The external control culture tells us to think of these symptoms as "conditions" over which we have very little control:

The phobic child avoids going to school <u>because</u> of his anxiety disorder.
The teenage girl loses interest in music and sports <u>because</u> of her depressive disorder.

Of course there's a powerful biological component to these responses. Think about our earlier discussion of temperament—the built-in emotional response style that we're born with. Some people are constitutionally disposed to respond to stress with anxiety, or depression, or with migraine headaches. But temperament does not determine behavior. That's such an important statement, that I'm going to repeat it.

> *Temperament does not <u>determine</u> behavior.*

Despite the built-in tendency to respond to stress in a particular physiological way, we can still choose thoughts and actions that lead to more effective total behavior, and these choices can change our physiology. If you are prone to depression, for example, you are free to choose to go to bed or go to the gym. One will affect your physiology quite differently than the other. You might even decide that medication is a good option for you, but you always have a choice. All of us have the responsibility to find an effective way to live, given the assets and liabilities of our physical and temperamental endowment.

It's important to view emotional symptoms as purposeful. Like all total behavior, they represent a "best attempt" to satisfy basic needs. Anxiety and depression are not the causes of a child's difficulties—they are an aspect of his attempt to restore balance and inner control.

So, how to best respond to a child's emotional symptoms? First, do your best not to become too emotionally reactive. Your child's emotionality should neither be indulged nor dismissed. If you view his symptoms as a best attempt, it will lead you in a helpful direction. Try to acknowledge the sense behind his intention—appreciating the real challenge that he's trying to face. You can express sympathy for his distress without conveying to him that he's an unfortunate victim. Always express confidence that, in time, he'll find a better way. Let him know that you're there to help him, not to bail him out.

Child: *"Mommy, please come up here and take me home. I just can't bear being at camp—I'm so upset, I can't stand it!"*

Mom: *"Sweetheart, I know you're upset. It must be very difficult for you to be away for so long."*

Child: *"It is, it is. Please come get me—I'm awake every night. I'm too depressed to sleep."*

Mom: *"I'm so sorry you're not sleeping well. Is there anything we can send that will help you be more comfortable?"*

Child: *"No, no. Just come get me, pleeease!"*

Mom: *"I know it's not easy for you, but I know that you can do it. You've done difficult things before, and I'm very proud of you for trying so hard."*

Child: *"I really am trying my best, but it's just too much for me."*

Mom: *"Being away is not easy, I know. I'm very proud of you for trying your best. Should we talk again in a couple of days? I'm not sure if talking on the phone helps or hurts?"*

Child: *"Oh, yes, please, the unit director said that if I keep going to activities, I can call home again on Friday."*

Mom: *"That's great sweetheart. I look forward to talking with you. I love you."*

Child: *"I love you mommy, bye."*

A Better Explanation

Parents need more than a diagnostic label. They need a practical explanation of behavior that leads to a specific plan of action. When you use the principles of choice psychology to think about your child's behavior, you'll ask more *what* questions than *why* questions. And they will naturally lead you to a coherent plan of intervention:

1) *You will recognize the sense in your child's behavior—in the intention behind his choices.*
2) *You will favor belonging over power, and that will strengthen the connection between you.*
3) *You will encourage your child to generate more effective ways of getting what he wants most.*
4) *You will convey a sense of confidence in your child's own capability to balance his various needs, and make responsible choices.*

These are the keys to parenting by choice. Instead of stopping, suppressing, or controlling behavior, you connect with your child through understanding and encouragement. With that strong relationship to draw on, your child is better prepared to generate new behavior as he needs it—to choose better ways to satisfy his various needs for power, belonging, freedom, and fun.

14. ANXIETY AND SEPARATION PROBLEMS

JOSIE

Eight-year-old Josie was afraid to sleep in her own bed. Most nights, after a period of stalling, complaining, and crying she would wait in her room until her older sister had gone to bed. Then, blanket in tow, she would sneak into her sister's room and camp out on the floor. At other times, when her sister resisted, Josie would squeeze into her parents' bed. Everyone in the family was tired of this routine, but somehow they put up with it. It seemed easier to give in than to endure an annoying emotional performance.

Josie's parents argued over the best way to respond to their daughter's problem. It was the classic protect vs. prepare disagreement. Mrs. Lombardi was more indulgent than her husband and was reluctantly willing to allow their daughter to come sleep in their bed. She believed that Josie had always been sensitive, and to push her out could be overwhelming. "She'll sleep in her own bed when she's ready," is how Mrs. Lombardi saw things. Even she realized, however, that Josie herself was troubled about her nighttime difficulty. Josie never had sleepovers, either at home or at friends' houses, and she had even missed a birthday party that was celebrated in this way.

Mr. Lombardi thought his wife was being foolish, and if they were tougher with Josie, she would rise to the occasion and be able to sleep on her own. "She'll do it if she has to," he reasoned. "She can't always depend upon us to cater to her; the real world won't be so accommodating!" Although he tried not to verbally admonish Josie, he slipped from time to time. She was well aware of his disapproval and disappointment in her.

Josie had always been sensitive. She was shy around strangers and inhibited in new situations. The Lombardi's were concerned that things appeared to be getting worse. Josie would insist that her family sit very near her when they watched a video or television program that was even mildly aggressive. Her parents could also see that she was nervous about play dates, apparently because they might include a frightening video game or movie. These were the reasons that the Lombardi's came to counseling and began to learn about choice parenting.

When apprehension, worry, and anxiety become such prominent features of a child's world that basic functions are compromised, the condition is considered a *disorder*. Research indicates that anxiety disorders are the most common psychiatric problem among children and adolescents (Mash, 2003). The total behavior of "being anxious" can take many forms; in young children of Josie's age, separation problems are the most common.

The Lombardi's knew that Josie had always been sensitive and timid in new situations. It was her temperament; she came that way. Parents of children with anxious temperament have a delicate task on their hands. They must encourage their children to be fully engaged in the world and to develop a sense of inner control despite a physiology that is sending frequent danger signals.

DEGREES OF ANXIOUS TEMPERAMENT

LOW   HIGH

gregarious, adventurous.........friendly, easy-going.........cautious, inhibited

An anxious temperament is a dimensional characteristic, not an illness. Everyone has a tendency to respond to novelty with some apprehension, but people differ in the degree of that response. Those who are very low on this dimension are more gregarious but also run the risk of being reckless in their judgment. They don't have the benefit of mild anxiety to give them caution when it is warranted. Those who are very high on this dimension, like Josie, tend to be more inhibited in new situations. They are also at some risk of being overly cautious, and even avoidant to a self-defeating degree. It is important to remember, though, that temperament doesn't determine behavior. Despite an anxious temperament, one can choose to be socially engaged and even somewhat adventurous.

Being Anxious

The physiology of anxiety is an arousal of the autonomic nervous system, which readies us to face survival emergencies. Sometimes referred to as the "fight or flight" response, it brings a keyed-up feeling along with such physical responses as sweating, dry mouth, trembling, nausea, muscle tension and restlessness. This physical set actually comes in handy when we're trying to escape a wild boar. Of course there aren't a lot of boar in most of our lives, but our physiology doesn't know that. The thinking part of the total behavior "being anxious" can include worrying and jumping from thought to thought, or scanning.

The Total Behavior, "Being Anxious"

Acting	**Thinking**
avoiding, complaining..	worrying, fretting…
Feeling	**Physiology**
being nervous, upset…	being tense, restless..

Josie may feel some apprehension during her busy day, but probably has more trouble at night. Remember the total behavior suitcase? During an active day, Josie's action and thinking behaviors of playing, working, eating, and socializing override her anxious physiology. In essence, she chooses playing with her friends and doing well in school over being afraid.

In the evening when she settles down for bed, there are less external distractions, and Josie is more aware of her own physiology—the sensations in her body. Being alone in her bed is uncomfortable, and she begins to worry. Her total behavior of "being anxious" includes the thinking part,

> *"I can't handle this alone…I need someone stronger than me for comfort and safety."*

When she sneaks into her sister's room and curls up on the floor with her blanket, she feels relieved and safe. Over time, though, she thinks of herself as weak and not very worthwhile.

Choosing a Response to a Child's Anxiety

The choice parenting tools that are helpful for anxiety and separation problems include connecting, planning, and setting limits, but the most important part of your response is the attitude that lies beneath the techniques—confidence in your child's capability and competence. Your child is feeling out of control and powerless. Rather than carrying her suitcase where she wants it to go, she's being pulled around by one of its compartments—her own physiology. To help her regain a sense of power and control, you should convey a firm belief that she possesses the inner resources to handle this very difficult problem. It's very important that you acknowledge the difficulty she faces; that's how to engage the best emotional connection. Only if your child feels connected with you can she really benefit from the message of confidence that you convey. Remind her of your knowledge that she can do difficult things. She'll protest and disagree, but be steadfast. Even in the face of her doubt, you know that she can do it!

Mrs. L.:	*"I think it's time that we found a better way to handle bedtime, don't you?"*
Josie:	*"I don't want to talk about it."*
Mrs. L.:	*" I know; it's not easy. You have a tough time feeling comfortable at night, but I know we can find a better way to solve this" (Connecting).*
Josie:	*"I just can't get to sleep by myself—you have to let me stay in your room!"*
Mrs. L.:	*"I know you're having a hard time, but you can find a way to do this. Besides, Dad and I really want our privacy at night (Limits). Let's try to come up with a different way to help you."*
Josie:	*"It's no use—I won't be able to do it!"*
Mrs. L.:	*"It'll be hard at first, but I've seen you do difficult things before. We'll work it out."*

It wasn't easy for Josie's mom to convey this message of confidence. She also has an anxious temperament and sometimes doubts her daughter's ability to overcome a challenge. So, how do you convey confidence when you just don't *feel* it? You also have to learn to carry your own suitcase and not be tugged around by some part of it. It takes a decisive act of will to "act as though" you feel sure, even though you are not so sure. Think it, and act it, and your physiology will follow in time. That's the principle of total behavior.

If you over-respond to your child's plight by mirroring her upset or by assuming too much responsibility in the management of her difficulty, you will only reinforce her dependence. She may get her way in the short run, but she will ultimately feel weak, not powerful, because she's not achieving the solution that she wants most.

Using choice psychology as a guide, Mrs. Lombardi found the courage to set her own limit. When she was clear that she wanted privacy at night, she and her daughter were able to work out a better plan. Josie could knock on her parents' door and come in for a few minutes of reassurance anytime she felt she needed to. Her father learned to be supportive, not critical at these times. Big sister said it was O.K. for Josie to sleep on her floor now and then, but not every night. With these resources and limits in place, Josie rather quickly went about her business of getting used to being alone at night in her own room. Within two weeks she was pretty much there, spending only one or two nights a week with her sister. A month later, she attended her first birthday sleepover party!

In this family, connecting and limit setting helped encourage Josie to make changes in the thinking and activity parts of her total anxiety behavior. As she experienced more success and inner control, her anxious physiology quieted down, too.

Parenting a child with anxiety and separation problems is a very tricky balancing act. It requires that you connect by appreciating your child's challenge and also step back and allow her to choose effective coping behavior. Every summer I work with many parents who are getting distress calls from overnight camps. When they are able to strike a balance between connecting and setting their limits, their children generally find a better way to be at camp.

Common Pitfalls

Here are a few of the most common obstacles that parents encounter as they try to respond to their child's anxiety and separation problems:

1. <u>Practicality</u>

    It's very inconvenient to connect with an apprehensive child when you've got things to do and a schedule to keep. An emotionally connected conversation takes time and patience, and you're a busy person!

    → Give yourself a break; you can't always get it just right. But when you can, try to keep in mind that the connection with your child is more important than the practical matter at hand. Accept the fact that if you have a child with anxious temperament, you're often going to be late.

2. <u>Shame and Embarrassment</u>

    We all have pictures in our head of how our family "ought to look." If one or more of our children has difficult behavior, there's going to be quite a gap between that inner world and reality.

    → It takes a lot of courage to face that reality and to accept that you have little control over how you appear to others in the community. Some may judge you but, in truth, most people are too caught up with their own struggles to give a lot of thought to yours.

3.   Parent-to-Parent Conflict

It is so common for couples to differ on the prepare/protect debate. In reality, the fact that you have different perspectives can be a great asset to the family. If the two of you stay connected and try hard to appreciate the sense of the other's position, you will be able to reach agreements—and it will help your marriage, as well.

→ Try to keep in mind that there are many perfectly acceptable parenting styles. The really important dimension to keep your eye on is the degree to which you try to control your child's choices. You can run a tight ship with clear limits and still elicit plans and solutions from your child rather than dictating rules to him.

4.   Emotional Fusion

For many parents, this is the toughest challenge of all—trying to keep your emotional balance when your child has lost his. To help your child learn to cope better with his distress, you've got to be able to tolerate him being in distress. This is not easy. If you "can't stand" him being upset, you're liable to overprotect or manipulate to change him. In either case, he won't learn to generate his own effective behavior.

→ Find out what helps you cope with your child's distress. Maybe it's talking to your spouse or to a good friend, or perhaps just taking a walk. Get behind the idea that your child being in distress is not a tragedy; it's a natural part of life that he can and should learn to cope with.

Being Phobic

For some children, anxiety is expressed as a phobic response. This means that…

1)   The anxious behavior is highly focused on a specific object or setting, such as their school building, dogs, airplane travel, etc…

And…

2)   Tremendous effort goes into avoiding that object or setting.

Children who are being phobic get tremendous reinforcement for their avoidance behavior because of the dramatic reduction of anxiety when they do avoid. Because they are so invested in this avoidance strategy, the most important tool to help them is *encouraging self-evaluation.* They've got to become aware that their current method of coping is self-defeating before they will be courageous enough to try new thoughts and actions.

> *Mark is a twelve-year-old boy who has struggled with anxiety all of his life. He is socially inhibited, gives up easily in the face of new challenges, and has come to think of himself as "a loser." His mom, a single parent, has consulted with psychiatrists, and Mark has been on various medications with only minimal effect. Counseling has been useful, especially in helping him understand his own emotional response style and thereby providing some measure of control over his difficulties. His mother noticed some progress in the past year as Mark allowed himself to take a few chances. With modest academic and social successes, his self-esteem began to improve. Unfortunately, as he entered middle school, Mark became extremely preoccupied with a school bully. Although he was never physically attacked, Mark was the victim of some mild taunting. His intensified anxious behavior was now organized around coping with this menace, and his primary strategy was avoidance. Mark would hide out in a remote hallway and arrive at his classes late in order to avoid an encounter with this feared classmate. He also passed up a school dance for the same reason, and hated himself for his cowardice. He maintained that he was unable to face this bully and that he would always be a loser. He said this was the worst time of his life.*

What a difficult challenge this young man was facing. The middle school years are fraught with social challenges, and a boy like Mark who is unsure of himself and not socially skilled is sure to feel way in over his head. Fearing the bully was probably Mark's best attempt to gain some measure of control over a swirling torrent of inadequacy and uncertainty. He wasn't the only one who was struggling; Karen, his mother was distraught.

> *When we spoke, Karen told me how difficult it was for her to see her son being cowardly. She felt terrible for him but confessed that she was very angry, too. She wanted him to be more courageous, to confront his fears. She believed that this was the only way he could get better, and she feared that he might always be a weak and ineffective person. As Karen conducted her own self-evaluation (What am I doing? How is it working?), she acknowledged that her dealings with Mark alternated between regretful indulgence and angry insistence. She had lost her way.*

Karen didn't have a clear game plan, but she needed one to be effective with her very challenging son. Karen's anger was part of her unsuccessful effort to change Mark. That kind of critical attitude is nearly always self-defeating.

Whenever Mark sensed his mother's disapproval, he either became dejected and withdrawn, or he would lie. He would tell her that it had been a good day, with little anxiety or avoidance. In this way he could avoid feeling like such a disappointment.

Anxiety is a very private event, and unless your child is willing to share his experience with you, you won't be of much help to him. First, you've got to connect. Then, you can encourage some self-evaluation. And finally, you can very gently plan new behavior together.

For Karen to reconnect with Mark around this problem, she had to change the way she thought about his avoidance behavior. She had to respect it as Mark's current best attempt, rather than convey a critical, *"I can't believe you did that,"* attitude. This was really the toughest part for Karen. She realized that her own critical attitude was her best attempt to control a situation that really scared her, and she was afraid that if she *"let up,"* she would be surrendering to his phobia, and encouraging it to flourish. That's the control imperative at work—when we don't have effective control, we tend to act more controlling, even if it doesn't help.

Karen was driving Mark to a before-school meeting for a club he wanted to join. As they pulled into the parking lot, a group of students were walking by and came very close to the car. Mark suddenly dove down below the dashboard, hiding. After the students passed by, he tentatively emerged. Karen tried a different approach:

Karen: *"That was a tough moment."*
Mark: *"Don't say anything mom, please. I know it was stupid."*
Karen: *"Well, I don't know if it was stupid; I guess you did what you needed to."*
Mark: *"I did—I had to. I thought he might be there. Did you see him?"*
Karen: *"I didn't really notice. Are you O.K.?"*
Mark: *"Yeah, I'm O.K. mom."*
Karen: *"I guess sometimes you just feel like you have to hide."*
Mark: *"I don't do it all the time, really. They just surprised me, that's all."*
Karen: *"Yeah I could see that. Well, did it help?"*
Mark: *"I guess so, in a way. But I don't really want to hide so much. It's so babyish."*

In this exchange, Karen successfully inhibited her impulse to be critical. Instead, she tried hard to see the sense in Mark's behavior, and to acknowledge it. That's a very good way to stay connected. She went on to encourage self-evaluation when she asked, *"did it help?"* When Mark said that *he* doesn't want to hide so much, he was preparing himself for the possibility of new behavior. Karen needn't remind him that *she* doesn't want him to hide so much—he's acknowledged it as his own goal. At another time, their conversation moved a little further along:

Mark: *"I'm not sure I want to be in the chess club."*
Karen: *"It's not easy for you to be in activities at school, I know."*
Mark: *"I know I shouldn't avoid it, but it's just too hard. What if I get really nervous and do something stupid? You think I should do it, I know."*
Karen: *"Look, you're trying very hard to be more involved at school, and I'm very proud of you."*
Mark: *"I'm just not sure that I'm really a club kind of guy. Other people do it so easily!"*
Karen: *"I know; some things are harder for you. Is there any other way you can handle this without avoiding it?"* (Planning together)
Mark: *"Well, I'm worried that if I really join, and want to quit later, you won't let me. That's happened before."*
Karen: *"You'd like to try it for a while, but reserve the right to drop out later? O.K., that seems fair to me."*
Mark: *"You won't be mad?"*
Karen: *"I'll try my best. I think I can do it."*

This is a wonderful exchange, in that Mark is now asking his mom for new behavior that's not easy for her! It's a great opportunity for Karen to demonstrate that we all have our struggles, and that all we can do is try our best.

The shift from controlling to connecting that Karen made was very important for her and her son. She had a clearer game plan to follow, and so she felt more "in control" and less stressed and angry. Mark hasn't suddenly become a socially comfortable child, and he hasn't given up his reliance on avoidance as a coping strategy. But he is progressing nicely, becoming more socially engaged, and consequently more confident and self-accepting. And he did very well on the chess team—for the entire season.

15. AGGRESSION AND DISRUPTIVE BEHAVIOR

Aggressive behavior is the hallmark of external control psychology. It represents an attempt to solve problems by imposing one's will on others and pressuring them to do what you want. Childhood aggression can take many forms. These include hostile and threatening remarks, oppositional and defiant challenges, damage to objects and property, and outright physical violence. Stealing and lying can be equally disruptive. In all of these cases, a child relies on pressure and externally imposed control in order to bring his worlds into balance. He's trying hard, as we all do, to bring the real world into alignment with his inner pictures of wants and needs. He needs power, and he wants things his way. His aggression is a poor strategy, however, because of the toll it takes on important relationships with parents, friends, teachers, and coaches. He may need power, but he also needs love and belonging. Nonetheless, the child persists because his aggression is at least marginally satisfying.

Aggression is satisfying because it produces some measure of power in the experience of the offender. The aggressor is calling the shots and making things happen. It's not so much the "negative attention" that's motivating but the fact that he's effecting a reaction in others. There's a sense of power and control when he finds he can make others squirm. It's only marginally satisfying, though, because his controlling ways are highly disconnecting. Most highly aggressive kids I work with are very unhappy that important people in their world are annoyed with them, but they seem curiously unimpressed by the idea that their own controlling behavior might have something to do with it.

Marginally satisfying aggressive behavior, left unchecked, usually progresses to more serious levels. What begins as a hostile and threatening attitude can well become overtly abusive behavior.

Children who rely on aggression to satisfy their needs for power and self-worth are generally not having a pleasant time themselves. They don't feel particularly successful and often believe that other children have an easier time than they do. They may be right. Many aggressive children were born with difficult temperaments, such as high distractibility and impulsivity, and their style can elicit negative reactions from peers who find it annoying. Aggressive children sense the social tension but have no idea how to improve things. Parents of such action-oriented children are perpetually correcting them, but again, the children do not feel as if they have effective control over the behavior they are being asked to change. The parent-child struggle that ensues has been described as "*mutual*

training in aversive responding (Hinshaw, p. 175)," as the frustrated parents punish and the struggling children resort to increasingly aggressive behavior.

The key to changing this pattern of aggressive conduct is self-evaluation and
awareness. As with any important behavioral change, it occurs only when the person exhibiting the behavior becomes impressed that it is essentially self-defeating
and resolves to try new behavior. Aggressive kids are typically not very reflective
and often seem "allergic" to this kind of self-examination. They find it too
uncomfortable and even painful to consider that they are perpetuating their own
difficulties. As we discussed earlier, punishment is not a very effective way to
increase children's self-awareness. Instead, it encourages angrier and/or sneakier
behavior. With the tools of choice psychology, we can find better answers.

> *JEFF*
> *Jeff Anderson was described to me as an impulsive, abrasive, unhappy four-
> teen-year old. I was told that he excelled at nearly every sport he tried, did
> only fairly well in school, and wasn't very popular with other kids. He was
> also treating his younger brother very badly. His parents, John and Beverly,
> told me on the phone they wanted to bring Jeff in to see me—"to find out
> what is really bothering him."*
>
>> *"We don't get it; this kid has a great life. We give him everything, and
>> he's so ungrateful. He always wants something more, and he just push-
>> es and pushes until he wears us down and one of us gives in, or
>> explodes. We're always fighting—with him and with each other."*
>
> *I suggested they tell Jeff they were coming in to talk with me about improv-
> ing things and that they'd like him to come along. I told them not to push
> too hard, not to fight with him about it. Beverly told me that this approach
> would definitely not work because Jeff would be sure to refuse. I told her
> that it couldn't fail because the idea was to allow him his own choice. They
> reluctantly agreed and came in to see me soon afterward, without their son.*
>
> *The Andersons were very nice people, but they were very worn down. They
> told me that Jeff had always been a difficult child, but lately things were
> really getting out of hand. I asked how the conversation about the appoint-
> ment had gone, and John said,*
>
>> *"All right, I guess. We did what you said—gave him the choice, and
>> of course he got kind of nasty with us and said, 'No f...ing way!' We*

*didn't fight, so he's not here. But we can't always give him what he
wants, right? After all, I don't always get what I want."*

*The important thing here is that John and Beverly chose not to fight about
the appointment with Jeff, and they were successful. I agreed with them that
their son can't always have things his way, but I pointed out that even when
he is frustrated and upset, they can always choose not to fight with him.*

One of the most important ideas to keep in mind when you're dealing with "difficult people," is to try not to be controlled by them. After all, the thing that
makes them difficult is that they so often resort to control maneuvers in order to
get their needs met. By the way, Jeff probably sees his parents as difficult people
and feels as though he's resisting their control. When you find yourself fighting
all the time, like the Andersons said they were, then there's a lot of mutual controlling going on. If you're unhappy about fighting, you may be telling yourself,
"He's making me do it." You've succumbed to an external control psychology and
given your child way too much power. Stop fighting. It's doing serious damage to
the cord that connects you, and there are better ways to parent. Regardless of how
adept at control-maneuvering your child is, you can nearly always choose not to
fight. It's a very important first step, and the Andersons showed me that they
could do it.

Some of my favorite things to say instead of fighting:

- *"I'm trying hard not to fight with you."*
- *"I really don't want to have an argument."*
- *"I'm not going to fight about this; maybe we can talk about it later?"*

*In our meeting, I learned more about Jeff's behavior. His parents found him
to be hostile and unhappy. He was generally very focused on some new video
game or piece of sports equipment that he wanted them to buy for him, and
he was remarkably persistent. If they did buy it, he'd often mistreat it and
promptly move on to a new toy that he "had to have." If his parents elected
not to buy the desired item, he'd make everyone's life miserable by cursing,
pushing, and breaking things. In the last several months, there was more
overtly aggressive behavior. Jeff was physically pushing his younger brother
around to the point of hurting him. He had also pushed his mother, and
during a recent argument with his dad, he had spit in his face.*

The Andersons had tried a lot of things to try to help Jeff and to stop the oppressive behavior. They punished him, usually by grounding "until further notice." Of course, whichever parent was not the current target of Jeff's hostility would usually relent after a day or two. They also tried to make deals with Jeff, such as "we'll get you that new equipment if you agree to be better around the house." Invariably, he would soon want something more and resort to demanding and other forms of pressure and coercion. Jeff's parents admitted they often pushed back, saying some very ugly and insulting things to Jeff. They weren't happy about their own actions, but they were hard-pressed to find any way to get through to him.

John and Beverly were arguing a lot with each other about how to manage Jeff. At any given time, one of them was more a target for Jeff's hostility and would usually react with impatience and hostility. The other would favor more conciliation, which would upset the targeted one even more. John told me that being spit at by his son was incredibly painful to him. It made him realize how very far off base they were, and that they needed some serious help.

> *"He doesn't really seem to care about us at all. I don't know how to get through to him. We're thinking of taking away his sports activities—it seems like the only thing he cares about. Should we do that? I just don't know."*

The Anderson's situation was pretty tough, because when this kind of control maneuvering has gone on for so long, the cord of connection is badly worn. That's why the "deals" that they'd tried to make with Jeff hadn't worked. The ability to make and keep agreements is fundamental to every healthy relationship, but Jeff was unwilling to keep his agreements with his parents. Instead, he was relying on the imposition of power to meet his wants and needs. Remember, aggressive behavior unchecked tends to progress and escalate. Although Jeff was most disruptive at home, his hostility was spilling out into other areas. He was increasingly getting into trouble with teachers and coaches, and despite his athletic prowess, he was becoming less popular with his teammates. As Beverly explained sadly, "the phone just doesn't ring for him."

Jeff's compulsive interest in acquiring toys and things is quite striking, and a clue to the fact that some other basic need is seriously unfulfilled. John and Beverly have a good idea of what was troubling Jeff most. They understood that he was very hurt about being unpopular, and that it must not have been easy for him to see his young brother enjoying his many friendships. They were sure that if he would simply treat people more kindly, he'd be more successful socially. Certainly they could spend a lot of time (and money) trying to get to the bottom of "what's really wrong with Jeff," but from a choice psychology perspective, they've already got quite a bit of information. They know that their son is making the best attempt he knows of to satisfy his basic needs but his effective control of *belonging* is very poor. He's a bright boy and could probably learn more about how to make friends, but at the moment he really isn't interested in accepting help from others. That makes the *planning together* tool a poor option, at least for the time being.

> *I talked with the Andersons about a two-track approach for their problem: strengthening the relationship (staying connected), and managing the aggressive conduct (setting your limits, specials on hold). After their own parent self-evaluation, they were quite ready to try something new and different.*

> *Strengthening the cord: The idea here was simple: John and Beverly should try to engage in activities with Jeff that they would each find enjoyable. At the same time, it was important they stop when they were no longer enjoying the activity and they try very hard not to fight about it.*

> *Beverly quickly identified nighttime chats that she often had with Jeff as her opportunity. As she learned more about choice psychology, she realized that the "sermonizing" that she sometimes included in these chats was disconnecting, and she resolved to stop doing it. Instead, when Jeff did mention some questionable activity that he or a friend was engaged in, Beverly began to ask what he thought about it. The toughest part was breaking away when she no longer wanted to talk. If Jeff wasn't ready to stop, he would usually insist and use anger and upset to coerce his mother to continue. Beverly learned to say,*

> > *"Let's agree on how much more time, because I'm really ready to go do some other things."*

> *Of course Jeff would quickly agree to five more minutes, with no apparent intention of honoring the agreement. At the end of the time, Beverly would leave, saying something like,*

> > *"O.K., I really meant it. I'm going to go now."*

The hardest part was walking away silently while Jeff was cursing.

John's opportunity was very similar, but instead of chatting, it involved throwing a ball in the yard. This was something that Jeff was usually interested in doing and each of them found it to be enjoyable. The problem was, Jeff never had enough. When John wanted to stop, Jeff wouldn't permit it. The new approach was much the same as what his wife was doing—agree on a limit, stick to it, try not to fight, and avoid the easy opportunity to point out Jeff's shortcomings as he displayed them. Instead of saying,

> *"You see, this is why nobody wants to play with you,"*

John learned to say,
> *"I know that you're not happy about it, but I really am going to stop now."*

This isn't easy to do when the boy you raised is calling you a fat pig! Nonetheless, John did his best.

The Andersons were doing an excellent job of connecting rather than fighting with Jeff. You can see they even found some opportunities for *encouraging self-evaluation* and *planning together*. They were learning not to take the bait, not to participate in a coercive relationship. Again, that's the key to being involved with a difficult person—staying connected without being controlled by their behavior. If Jeff was some neighbor down the street, John and Beverly probably wouldn't have anything to do with him—his behavior is just too offensive. But when the difficult person is someone you love, someone you choose to be involved with, you need a better answer.

KEYS TO LIVING WITH DIFFICULT PEOPLE

- **Stay Connected**; Try not to criticize or fight.

- **Don't Be Controlled by Their Behavior**; Set your limits, and walk away.

- **Get Some Support**; Find a friend or partner you can "debrief" with—tell them how hard you're working.

As a practicing psychologist I've learned that the clearest picture of problem behavior is often revealed after you begin to make an intervention. As John and Beverly pursued their plan for staying connected with Jeff, it became all too apparent why he has so much trouble connecting successfully with other kids. Jeff has a strong tendency for "negative persistence," which is simply a way of describing his dogged determination of his wants, despite the wants of others. He is not "antisocial" or disinterested in the feelings of others—he really does care about his family and friends. He just finds it very difficult to be mindful or aware of their needs while he is in need. This blind spot for social reciprocity is very common in kids with even mild learning disabilities or attention deficits. For Jeff, it may be part of the reason that he's so successful athletically—he plays aggressively and is not intimidated by his opponent's efforts. For Jeff to become more socially successful, he'll need to take more responsibility for understanding and working with his temperament. But he won't be interested in taking that step as long as he's stuck in a behavior style of coercion and intimidation.

> _Specials on hold:_ *When a child is breaking things and hurting people, a very clear and strong response to this "unsafe" behavior is called for. Jeff's aggressive behavior was so widespread that the simple removal of a game or privilege would be ineffective. Instead, I spoke with John and Beverly about a more ambitious application of specials on hold, the introduction of a "status level system."*
>
>> *There are two levels of status, high and low. On high status, the child enjoys all of the special privileges that life in the family usually brings. Television, video games, transportation to stores and events, etc...As long as he is not physically offending anyone (hitting, spitting, pushing, damaging property), he remains on high status.*
>>
>> *On low status, there are no special privileges. Only the basics are provided. Special foods, electronic games, and expensive toys are removed. Beyond school and health-related appointments, transportation is also withheld. This is not easy to do, but with a little creativity and a locked cabinet or two, many families have found a practical way to engage low status.*
>>
>> *The child controls the status level he is on. He receives one warning for unsafe behavior, and continued aggression results in the start of low status. The child remains on low status until he is able to maintain two days of safe behavior.*

The proper parental attitude is essential for success and to prevent this from feeling like another angry punishment. Parents should respond without undue negative emotion. They should be "in the child's corner," optimistic and encouraging that he'll be able to return to high status soon.

After discussing these basics with the Andersons, John and Beverly fashioned their own application of the specials on hold level system. They decided that on low status, there would be no television or video games. But more importantly, they decided that Jeff should not participate in sports teams while on low status. This was a difficult decision for them, but they included their son's baseball coach in the process. He assured them that he would cooperate and would try not to penalize Jeff for an absence due to low status.

The two-track approach worked very well. John and Beverly were learning to be less controlled by Jeff's angry provocative behavior. They pushed back a lot less often, and this resulted in more opportunity for useful conversations. Jeff only went on low status once, after repeatedly pushing his brother. The procedure didn't eliminate his angry, difficult attitude, but the more severe and unsafe behavior was gone. And then a very interesting thing happened. Jeff decided that he wanted to talk to me. He had some "complaints" about the way his parents were using these new methods.

Jeff told me that he wasn't the only aggressive one in the family—that his father said some pretty mean things to him when he got angry, and he didn't lose any privileges! I validated his observations and told him that I was trying to help his parents chose less angry and controlling ways to respond. I also suggested that he might want his own place to talk about getting along with family and friends. He said he'd think about it.

The healing process for the Andersons was slow and steady. A clear limit about unsafe behavior had been well established, and that allowed more opportunity for other issues to come to light. Jeff began talking to his school counselor about his social difficulties and began having more success in that area. His parents had a much better game plan to deal with Jeff's negative persistence, and their relationship was less turbulent and more connected. It was becoming increasingly apparent, however, that the Anderson's marriage was not in the best shape. They were no longer arguing about Jeff, but they were frustrated and unhappy about other aspects of their relationship. They had some new tools though, a new way to think about relationships using choice psychology, and they continue to use this approach to try to find a more satisfying way to be together.

This is not at all an unusual sequence of events. I think of it this way: *When the noise in the room is diminished, the important conversations are more clearly heard.* Some would say that Jeff's problems were masking what was "really" wrong in the family, an underlying marital conflict. Others would say that Jeff's "real" problem was his social inadequacy. My own belief is that this distinction between superficial and deeper, more important problems is nonsense. They are all different expressions of the same fundamental human problem, finding effective ways to meet our basic needs. All we can really respond to is one another's behavior, and if we do that with care and concern, the noise will diminish, and other important conversations can begin.

16. DEPRESSION AND UNDER-FUNCTIONING

DAVE

Dave Seltzer was a sensitive and bright thirteen-year-old boy who was seeing a psychiatrist friend of mine for the treatment of depression. Dave was feeling hopeless and overwhelmed, was missing quite a bit of school, and was spending a lot of time in bed. He and his father argued a lot about his passivity and lack of effort. My colleague had treated the boy's mother for depression in the past, and he viewed Dave's primary problem as an inherited mood disorder. Consequently, he prescribed antidepressants, which were having only a limited effect. He wisely saw that the parents' attitude was an important part of Dave's treatment, and he referred the family to me for some exposure to choice psychology. The Seltzers came readily to my office for family counseling and guidance.

Dave's mom told me that her son did a lot of complaining and a lot of crying. She'd heard him say things like, "What's the use of going on…it all seems so pointless." Naturally, this frightened her. Like her son, Mrs. Seltzer had a sensitive temperament and could well relate to what he was going through—perhaps too well. She could listen to his complaints for a while and try to be supportive, but before long she found it quite overwhelming and would distance herself by getting more involved with her work.

Mr. Seltzer was very concerned about his son's future and the damage being done by all of the missed school and poor grades. He realized that Dave was having a hard time but couldn't understand why he didn't try harder to get himself going. Mr. Seltzer was a practical and impatient man and tended to push his son, reminding him of his responsibilities and warning him that the quality of his schoolwork over the next few years was crucial to a successful future.

Dave was very upset by his father's demands. He viewed his dad as insensitive and inhuman, and frequently mentioned how much he hated him. They argued all the time. Mr. Seltzer didn't know how to get his son moving—to get him out of bed or to do some homework. Mostly, he pushed and yelled. Dave was often belligerent, calling his father a robot, saying that he was useless, laughing at him, etc…This was pretty hard for Mr. Seltzer to take, and he frequently pushed back, hard.

101

When I met with Dave, I was struck by his hopelessness. He felt over-whelmed and unable to meet the demands of his busy life—a challenging academic schedule and various music lessons and rehearsals. He was certainly quite angry about the hard time his dad was giving him. But the issue that he seemed most deeply troubled by was his lack of social success at school. Dave was really an intellectual and not particularly attuned to the popular culture. He hadn't found anyone else with whom to have the kind of conversations that came naturally to him. He certainly didn't fit in with the cool crowd, and other kids that he had been friendly with in earlier years seemed like total strangers today. He didn't have anything to say to them. He didn't feel he had much of a place at all.

"We have a lot of questions," Mr. Seltzer said to me. "Is our son truly depressed? We see him enjoying some activities, like going to his music lessons and playing video games online. Is he unable to do schoolwork because of an illness, or should we be pushing him to try harder?"

Many ways

There are many different ways that children express their unhappiness. Some kids are angry and disruptive, others are anxious and avoidant. Still others, like Dave, are depressive and under-functioning. Their pain is expressed through passivity and failure to meet basic responsibilities. Emotional pain is always caused by an inability to effectively satisfy one or more of the basic needs. More often than not, the effective balancing of love and power is the stumbling block. The specific form that a child's unhappiness takes, the *total behavior* of being angry, or anxious, or depressed, is not really the important element to focus on. In some ways, it's a smoke screen that diverts attention from the really important work that must be done—that the child learns to effectively meet his emotional needs and balance them with the needs of the people he cares about. By giving these symptoms of unhappiness descriptive labels, such as "anxiety disorder" or "mood disorder," we make possible an unfortunate logical error. It's easy to assume that what's wrong with Dave is that he "has depression," when in fact his depressive underfunctioning is his current best attempt to regain inner control and emotional balance. He's "being depressed" because he knows how, and as painful as this way of living is, it seems to be a better option than trying unsuccessfully to be social.

> **Psychiatric symptoms are a child's current best attempt to regain inner control and emotional balance.**

I don't mean to imply that psychiatric disorders don't exist, or that there's no such thing as clinical depression (major affective disorder). Here's what I mean. We all respond to stress and need-frustration differently. Some have strong inherited traits that predispose their physiology to depress. That physiological part of total behavior can be very powerful and can lead the thinking, feeling, and acting parts to follow along with it. But that powerful force can be overcome. It is possible to make an effective plan to overcome the physiology of depression by acting and thinking differently. Some people choose to use medication or holistic supplements to assist their effort, while others would rather not, perhaps finding the side effects to be unacceptable. In either case, the key to an effective recovery is the recognition that "depression" is not an external force of nature. It is an internally generated response, a total behavior over which we really can achieve greater control.

This important shift from external to internal choice psychology led the Seltzers to a very different response to their son's underfunctioning.

> *Mrs. Seltzer felt overwhelmed by her son's "illness." When she began to view his underfunctioning as total behavior, it allowed her to consider that other responses might be available to him. It wasn't easy, but in time she began to realize that Dave was capable of doing better—of finding better ways to meet his needs. The tools that were most important for her to use were Stay Connected, and Set Your Limits. The best she had to offer her son was her love and genuine regard for him, and her confidence that he had the inner resources to do better. She learned to set limits about how much complaining and negative talk she was willing to listen to. She learned to say things like,*

>> *"You know, Dave, I think I'm going to take a break. I don't really want to listen to so much complaining about your schoolwork."*

The big change was that she felt more in control, less overwhelmed, and consequently, she came back. Selective disengagement can actually be a very effective way to stay connected!

> *Mr. Seltzer was incredibly frustrated with his son's passivity. Feeling ineffective himself, he resorted to overpowering Dave with demands and criticism. Of course this was so disconnecting that his son ignored any advice he offered. The tools that were most important for Mr. Seltzer to use were Stay Connected and Plan Together. He had to find a new way of talking with his son about his responsibilities that wasn't so critical and disconnecting.*

He and I role-played together, so I could model a new way of talking with his son about his schoolwork:

Dr. P., as Dad: "So, have you got much work to do tonight?"

Mr. S., as Dave: "Who knows?"

Dad: *"I guess you don't feel much like schoolwork, huh?"*

Dave: *"Brilliant deduction!"*

Dad: *"I think it's important that you do <u>something</u>; what do you think?"*

Dave: *"Yes I suppose so, but I really can't. Not right now. Maybe later. Go away."*

Dad: *"Look, I really don't mean to push you, but I mean it. Doing something would be a good idea. What part of your work do you think you could do tonight?"*

Dave: *"Geez, get off my back will you? I can't do <u>anything</u> right now."*

Dad: *"I'm not going to fight with you about it, but I believe you can do <u>something</u>. I'll check back with you later."*

There's nothing harder to deal with than passivity. It's like trying to play catch with someone who's invisible. You really can't insist that the passive one engage with you. The best you can do is convey your interest in connecting, be careful not to create more distance with anger and criticism, and don't be afraid to take a break and come back later. Dave gave his father very little to engage with him about, except his underfunctioning. In this way, all of the family energy was focused on the fighting between Dave and his dad. If Mr. Seltzer could learn not to fight with his son, but at the same time maintain his expectation of responsible behavior, then Dave would eventually become engaged because he, too, is dissatisfied with the current state of affairs. Dave was trying to externalize the problem with his provocative underfunctioning, but if no one took the bait, he just might muster the courage to try a different response.

Fortunately, Dave was willing to go for counseling himself. In his sessions, he was learning about the total behavior of depression and was being coached to choose something different than the passive response that his physiology was offering. Complaints about his parents were met with the observation that they seemed to be trying some new behavior. After some time passed, Dave agreed that there was some movement on their part, and he began to talk about what he could do differently about his own unhappiness.

It was a gradual process, but over the course of several months, there was a lot less arguing between Dave and his dad. Dave was having more social success too; he found a way to become part of a lunchtime group, and even began a special friendship with a girl who he described as "smarter than me!" After that, he never missed another day of school.

His parents were delighted, if somewhat mystified about their son's steady recovery. Of course there was really nothing mysterious about it. Dave was getting better because he was choosing more effective behavior. But he was only able to do that once his parents became less of a hindrance and more of a support. When his mother was less overwhelmed by his symptoms, he was more willing to believe that he could do better. When his father stopped arguing and criticizing, Dave was able to focus on creating some reasonable plans for himself.

"He hasn't become a different person," Dave reported to me about his dad, "but he is a whole lot easier to live with."

Of course it would have been possible to use *Specials On Hold* to respond to Dave's failure to complete schoolwork and frequent absences. As mentioned earlier, this tool is rather heavy-handed and should really be deferred until the other tools have been given a fair chance. I find that controlling interventions such as sanctions and loss of privileges are used far too often, due to an anxious parent's sense of helplessness and desperation. Parents really do underestimate the power of their relationship with their children. They are surprised that when they shift their focus to repairing the connection, their children become more responsible about managing their work and relationships.

The Basics

When is it time to use the heavy guns? After all, there has to be a limit to what you allow, right? In my work with parents and children, I talk to them about *the basics,* referring to a <u>small</u> set of responsibilities that are really non-negotiable. For me, the basics that make sense are *personal health and safety, safe relationships, and school.* I suggest you be crystal clear that these basic responsibilities are so important to you that you will go to great lengths to be sure that they are respected. For example, if one of your *basics* is in jeopardy, there really is no other issue that can be discussed until there is an effective plan or agreement in place. We'll talk more about this in the next section on adolescence, but I want to touch on it here because school avoidance is such a common way for kids to under function.

> ## THESE ARE <u>MY</u> BASICS:
>
> - *Self Care*
>
> - *Safe Relationships*
>
> - *Work and School*

It is very, very important not to allow your child to avoid attending school. This is not always easy, because some kids who are being depressed or phobic feel overwhelmed with the prospect of getting up and out in the morning. Let me just say that this is a critical line that you don't really want to cross. It is easy for a child to become accustomed to staying home, and the longer he does, the more difficult it will be to reintegrate with the social stream at school. I would much prefer to see a struggling child have some special accommodation at school—perhaps doing his work in the guidance office for example—than to be at home for an extended time receiving tutoring or home instruction. If a child persists in school avoidance despite a good effort on the part of his parents to use the less controlling tools of choice psychology, I do recommend using the heavy guns. Sometimes, *specials on hold* will help to turn things around. If the problem has gone on for some time, it might require the kind of *status level system* that the Andersons used with Jeff (Chapter 15). Do what ever you need to let your child know how important this issue is, and that…

"…in our family, we are serious about the responsibility to go to work and to school."

WHAT ARE _YOUR_ BASICS?

- _____

- _____

- _____

Try to remember that a child who is underfunctioning is not just "doing nothing." His behavior represents his current best attempt to manage his life in such a way that he feels in control. He's trying to balance his various needs, although he may not be doing a very effective job of it. He may be sleeping all morning or doing no homework, or leaving a big mess. Whatever his total behavior looks like, your job is to try to stay connected with him while gently encouraging something different. The best way to stay connected is to try hard to see the sense in what he's doing. Try to acknowledge that while his behavior is really not O.K. with you, you can understand how he's come to choose it. He'll probably maintain that there's no choice involved, and that he can't help but be this way. Be patient and have faith. You'll find that choice psychology is contagious. If you are persistent about your expectations, without reverting to excessive external control, your child will gradually become more self-evaluating and more responsible with his life.

17. THE CHALLENGE OF ADOLESCENCE

Many parents are unsure of their ability to do well during this challenging stage of life. Choice psychology offers a clear game plan that can make the challenge less daunting. It suggests that you,

- *Understand what your child is going through,*
- *Recognize that he's making his own best attempt to meet his basic needs,*
- *Try hard to stay connected while setting reasonable limits.*

First, let's dispel the big myth about adolescent chaos and disorder. In reality, most children and their parents do quite well during the teenage years. It is a time of rapid change and uncertainty, and a time when family relations are truly tested. But most kids and their parents navigate these waters well, with few emotional or behavioral crises and with little damage done to their relationships. I think the reason that adolescents are so often referred to as crazy or impossible is that this stage of life is so difficult for us—the parents. Teens are incredibly variable in their day-to-day functioning and also may be a lot less compliant and cooperative than at earlier ages. Because they are less under our control, we may be inclined to view them as "out of control." But they're just making their best attempt to satisfy and balance their various needs, and because so much is changing for them, that balancing act is not easy. Remarkably, most meet this challenge very well.

This is important to note because if you and your child are having difficulty, you shouldn't write it off as the "normal" course of adolescent craziness. A child who is generating emotional symptoms and distress is frustrated and unhappy. To respond in a helpful way, to connect more than control, you need to understand a few things about adolescent total behavior.

Adolescent Total Behavior

THINKING	ACTING
Formal Operations— Thinking more deeply about himself and his place in the world.	**Rebellion? Not really.** Need for freedom is directed increasingly outside of the family.
FEELING **Moodiness—** Emotional regulation system is still under construction.	**PHYSIOLOGY** **Rapid change.** Physical growth and hormonal changes are a lot to handle.

Feeling: Teenage Moodiness

"One moment he's upbeat and affectionate; the next moment he's sullen and surly. It's so unpredictable! Sometimes he wants to get close, but I'm still hurting from an insensitive remark he made just moments before. I really don't know how to respond."

Adolescents can sure be moody! One of the things their brains don't do well is a function called *emotional regulation.* Later, they'll be better able to even out the highs and lows of their feelings and maintain emotional balance in the face of upsetting or surprising events. But teenagers have yet to develop that ability. Their emotional responses swing widely, and frequently. They're facing complex challenges, but their equipment is still under construction.

Thinking: Formal Operations

Teenagers think differently than younger children. Their cognitive development allows them to perform what are known as *formal operations.* That's another way of saying that they can reflect and think more deeply about events that have passed or have yet to come. For example, one reason that social status is so important during this stage is that teenagers are now able to think about social status. A younger child, such as your ten-year-old daughter, might decide not to play with her friend Janie and will think to herself,

"I really don't like her, she's not much fun. I don't want to be her friend."

Whereas your thirteen-year-old daughter might decide not hang out with Janie and will think to herself,

> *"She's so uncool—what would people think if I hung out with her? That's <u>so</u> not me. I'm out of here."*

Of course your teenager is not only making judgments about others, she's evaluating herself in a way she never did before.

> *"What do they think of me—how do I look? Oh, I'm such a loser."*

This ability to reflect and evaluate is a very important cognitive tool, but coupled with a lack of experience and perspective, it's a bit hard to handle. Your teenager may be distant and self-absorbed at times, spending more time thinking about herself and about her place in the world. With her increasing capacity for abstract thought, her world has become more complex, and finding an effective balance among her various needs is quite a challenge.

Acting: Adolescent Rebellion, or Not?

All children have a need for freedom, but adolescents increasingly look outside of the family to explore and enjoy new activity. Their social world is more complicated, and more effort is required to maintain a satisfying sense of belonging. Because it's difficult to balance the demands of friendships and family, in many cases it's the family connection that receives less effort. Your child may feel he can afford to neglect this part of his world—his family isn't going anywhere. Your job as a Choice Parent is to find a way to stay connected, while showing a high degree of respect for his need for freedom and independence.

Many people will tell you that adolescents need to rebel—that they need to "push against" their parents' values and customs in order to discover their own identity. I don't find this to be true at all. There is no innate need for rebellion, but there certainly is a basic need for freedom and autonomy. Teenagers don't need to rebel and reject their connections with their families, but they may choose to do so if it's the only way to experience freedom.

> *Adolescent rebellion results from insufficient respect for the child's heightened need for freedom.*

Brett

Maggie and Sam were participants in a Choice Parenting seminar and talked about a "morning problem" with their fourteen-year-old son. They described Brett as a great kid, but very private and very stubborn. Bret was an excellent student but preferred to do his homework late at night. He would spend most of his evening "I.M.ing" friends and chatting on the telephone, and wouldn't buckle down to do his work until his socializing was complete. He usually settled into bed at around 11:30, and sometimes even later. Sam explained:

> *"It's really absurd. We try to wake him in the morning for school, and he's practically comatose. He's obviously not getting enough sleep. It's so much work to get him up, and then when he's running late, he blames us for not trying hard enough to wake him! I think that this staying up 'til all hours is crazy, but we're really trying to be choice parents. Are we supposed to let him be late and work it out himself?"*

The group asked Maggie and Sam for some more information. It seems that Brett wasn't really showing any other ill effects from his sleep habits—his health was fine, and he was doing very well in his class work. Brett seemed to have a pretty healthy social life as well. All in all, his parents were pleased with how he was doing but were really stuck on how to deal with the late nights and the morning fights.

Maggie and Sam posed a great question. They could see their son was not managing his evening time well, and they were wondering how much they should intervene. Adolescents are incredibly touchy about being corrected—Brett's parents were wise to be thoughtful before jumping in with rules and directives.

Many teenagers are very possessive about those late evening hours. It's a private, personal time when they can socialize, aided by the various electronic devices that are central to their culture. It can be a very effective time to satisfy both belonging and freedom needs. Still, they may need some help bringing other considerations into balance. For Brett, the imbalance emerged as irresponsibility about waking. He blamed his parents for the difficulty rather than reassessing his own self-management. Maggie and Sam should focus on the waking problem, rather than the bedtime, as this was the problem that they shared with Brett. They might use *planning together* and *setting your limits*, and let Brett decide whether his new plan would include adjusting his bedtime. This kind of respect for his needs for freedom and belonging, coupled with a reminder of other responsibilities, is a good strategy for success with most teenagers.

Why not be more direct about his failure to get enough sleep? The same question can be asked about a teenager's failure to wear proper clothing or his spending too much time playing video games. There's nothing wrong with expressing an opinion about these matters, and even planning together to establish some guidelines that seem reasonable. But when your child's ideas of what is reasonable differ from your own, how much control should you exercise? You're once again confronting the parents' paradox. A helpful way out of this puzzle is to remind yourself of *The Basics*.

Remember The Basics

There are many adages that express this idea:

> *Pick your spots.*
> *Don't sweat the small stuff.*
> *Choose your battles.*

In other words, there should only be a few issues that you're willing to go to the mat for. *The Basics* is a guideline that says…

> *There is a short list of rules that are so important to our family that if any of them are in jeopardy, we will focus all our efforts on that problem.*

I suggest that teenagers be given plenty of freedom, as long as they're meeting their basics. Here again is the list that makes sense to me. Please edit it to reflect your own priorities.

THE BASICS

- *SELF CARE—To keep yourself safe and physically healthy.*

- *SAFE RELATIONSHIPS—To treat others well, and to be well treated.*

- *WORK and SCHOOL—To make reasonable efforts to meet your obligations.*

- _____

- _____

Self Care

Parents must decide for themselves what constitutes healthy self-care. For some, a modicum of exercise is a requirement. Others can tolerate lethargy but would never permit a belly ring. Don't forget to pick your spots carefully, and to keep the connection as your top priority.

Drug and alcohol use by any child is clearly unsafe behavior. It's a mistake to get sidetracked with debates about legal hypocrisy or the benign effects of marijuana. Stick to the issue of "belonging with the family," and that this activity is something that you consider unsafe. In one family I worked with, the contentious fifteen-year-old son challenged his parents about their regular alcohol use. I observed that the boy was in effect proposing a plan, suggesting that it would be easier for him to "just say no" if his parents would forego their cocktails. They did, and he did.

Safe Relationships

Physical violence is clearly out of bounds, but emotional safety is also an important family value. Where do you draw the line? An unkind gesture or facial sneer can be hurtful, but probably should be ignored. Continual verbal abuse of a parent or sibling, however, may very well meet your criterion of an unsafe relationship. If so, it is an example of a child who is not meeting *the basics* and ought to be the primary focus of your parenting attention.

Work and School

We mentioned in the previous chapter that a child is responsible to meet the basic requirements of school. For me, this includes making a reasonable effort to attend school, pay attention, and complete assignments.

There are many children whose temperament and learning styles are a poor match for their regular classroom programs. These kids are often classified as "disabled," when in fact they are quite able to learn, but may need less conventional approaches. The challenge for their parents is to work hard to find the resources that will help, while never excusing their children from the responsibility to work hard. Remember that a child's self-worth is strongly tied to his success in work and school achievement.

THINK IT OVER, WRITE IT DOWN…

Think about each of *The Basics*, and write down any issues that concern you regarding your child's behavior.

SELF-CARE, My child _____

_____.

SAFE RELATIONSHIPS, My child _____

_____.

WORK and SCHOOL, My child _____

_____.

Getting back to Brett, the basic responsibility that he was not meeting well was getting himself ready for school. I suggested that Maggie and Sam tread lightly on the bedtime issue and use their *planning* and *limit-setting* tools to focus on Brett's morning routine. This was the assignment that they chose, and here's what Maggie reported at the third and final meeting of their parenting seminar:

> *"The conversation was a lot different than I thought it would be. I was prepared to set my limit and had this phrase all ready in my head—*
>> *'The morning is not going well; I don't want to work so hard to wake you up.'*
> *But when we began talking about it, Brett was surprisingly agreeable. I think we were both nervous that there'd be some ugly confrontation, but there wasn't. He did throw one control maneuver at me, and I was brilliant at not taking the bait! I think he said:*
>> *'Here it comes, what kind of pop psychology are you going to lay on me today?'*
> *I just smiled and said that I wasn't happy about the morning routine, and asked if he was. It was really more of a* self-evaluation *conversation, although that's not what I had planned or expected. It went really well. He said it's really hard for him to wake up but insisted that it has nothing to do with his bedtime. Since our talk, he's definitely making a bigger effort. He's still moaning and groaning in the morning, but he's not blaming us for his trouble—and we're trying to do less for him."*

Sam chimed in,

> *"You're forgetting an important part. Brett asked if I would take my shower earlier so the bathroom is free whenever he finally gets up. It's really not much of a problem, so I've been doing that. It seems to have helped. I also think he has been going to bed a bit earlier, but I don't dare mention it. I know that if we made a big deal out of that, forget it! He would have really dug in his heels."*

This is the best kind of outcome. The practical problem of *Brett waking up* has not been solved, but ownership of the problem has totally shifted. Brett even generated a plan that he thought would help. Sam did well to adjust his own morning routine. It's always a good idea to encourage this kind of responsibility by accepting a child's suggestion, if it is even remotely reasonable.

Isn't it interesting that Maggie was prepared with her *limit-setting* phrase but ended up very naturally using the *encourage self-evaluation* tool. She knows her choice psychology and is less wedded to a particular tool than to the general concepts of internal control and protecting the connection.

The initial barb that Brett tossed at his mother was a classic control maneuver. Maggie handled it beautifully. In my experience, the choice parent of an adolescent often has to dodge one or two bullets early in an encounter to enjoy a connected and productive conversation.

SECTION FOUR
CHOICE PARENTING F.A.Q.'S

By now, you've learned quite a bit about choice parenting and the internal control psychology that it is based on. Or maybe you're just skimming through the book, figuring the F.A.Q.'s. will give you the main idea. In either case, here are the questions that I'm asked most frequently in Choice Parenting seminars and counseling sessions. The responses provide a good review of the key concepts and some direction about how to begin the shift to choice parenting.

When you say "more connecting, less controlling," are you saying I should give my kids free reign?

Not at all. Every relationship has limits, and your child needs to know that to effectively belong in his family, he's got to find a way to respect its basic guidelines. One of your primary responsibilities as a parent is to clarify the limits of acceptable behavior. What most people don't understand is that this can be done very effectively without a lot of threats, ultimatums, and other control maneuvers. Parents have plenty of power—they don't have to throw it around to remind everyone. In fact, the more blatant your use of external control, the more harm you do to your emotional connection with your child. Since that connection is the real source of your influence, excessive control is self-defeating. Define reasonable limits with quiet confidence and with the realistic awareness that your kids will choose for themselves when to cooperate, and when not to. The more respectful you are of their basic needs, the more cooperative they'll choose to be.

O.K., I buy that. But I don't see how you can dismiss the use of punishment. What happens when they "choose" to disobey me? Shouldn't there be a serious consequence to misbehavior?

Of course there should, but there are more effective consequences than imposing an arbitrary penalty. Most parents punish because of their need for power and self-worth; it's their best attempt at being a competent, *responsible parent. Choice parenting provides another option. A serious conversation between parent and child about misbehavior <u>is</u> a consequence, and if the parent is able to stay connected while maintaining his limits, it is a very powerful consequence. Some kids actually plead with their parents for a concrete punishment, hoping to avoid more meaningful and uncomfortable accountability. I'm a strong advocate of "planning together," a technique that requires the child to generate a new way to handle the problem situation in the future. It's a more effective way to help children feel responsible for their choices than criticism, coercion or punishment.*

You have another technique in your new set of tools that you call "specials on hold." It sounds like a fancy way of saying "I'm taking away a lot of your good stuff!" Isn't that punishment?

Not exactly, but I understand your point—like punishment, it certainly is a very controlling intervention. "Specials on hold" is a tool that should be used sparingly, and only when you've really given "planning together" an honest effort. You need to be persistent; your child will be stubborn about giving up his old, troublesome behavior. You should be prepared for slips when you're working out a new plan with your child. It might take several rounds of self-evaluation and renewed planning before you get sustained improvement.

Of course there is a point when a more controlling intervention is required. When done correctly, "specials on hold" differs quite a bit from the way most people use punishment. First, it should never be a way of expressing anger or frustration; Second, an exit strategy should be clearly in the child's control—that is, as soon as he commits to a realistic and <u>acceptable</u> plan for improvement, the sanction should be over; and third, the parent's attitude should be one of cooperation and a desire to help.
Instead of saying,
 "There, that'll teach you. No more computer for you!"
The message should be,
 "I want you to get back online too. I'm sure we can come up with a better agreement for the Internet that we can both live with."

I've been really trying to "stay connected" with my daughter. I'm telling her what I think, asking her what she thinks, and doing a lot less yelling. The thing is, she's complaining that I'm acting "all fake." Yesterday she called me the Stepford Mom. I'm not sure how to respond?

Congratulations! This is a sure sign that you're really changing your behavior. The "less controlling" you is unfamiliar to your daughter. She's feeling a little unsteady, and her gentle insults are her way of gaining a sense of inner control. Why not laugh with her and acknowledge that it's all a bit unfamiliar to you, too. Don't be shy about telling her that you're tired of fighting, and that you're trying something new.

My son's teacher asked me if we've considered therapy to address his aggressive behavior. I really like the ideas in the seminar, but should I consult a mental health professional?

The principles and tools of choice parenting can help to improve nearly any child behavior problem. But there are some problems that definitely require professional intervention. You should <u>always</u> see a licensed mental health practitioner if there is a presence of dangerous behavior. This includes self-harm, talk or written notes about self-harm, drug or alcohol abuse, frequent physical fights or taunting, and destruction of property. Beyond this, you might also seek professional help if your own efforts to change disruptive or self-defeating behavior have proved unsuccessful. While most behavior problems can be resolved with the techniques of choice psychology, you and/or your child might require more intensive work to interrupt deeply entrenched patterns. Finally, you might choose to consult with a therapist to work along with you, to strengthen your effort to parent more effectively.

*When choosing a therapist, I strongly suggest that you seek a state-licensed professional. Your local mental health association can usually be found in the phone book and should have a referral service. Ask for someone who is experienced with child and family work. Talk with a few therapists on the phone. Tell them a bit about your situation, and ask what their approach might be. Be sure that you're comfortable with their expertise and their manner. It shouldn't be too difficult to find someone with a **cognitive-behavioral** background; this approach is compatible with the choice psychology that is presented here. You can also contact the William Glasser Institute (wglasser.com) to find out if there is a Reality Therapist in your area. That person has been specifically trained in choice theory and will be very familiar with the ideas in this book.*

I'm very excited about the new approach that I've been learning. I can see that things are already improving between my daughter and I. Unfortunately, my husband hasn't attended the workshop! He's a

wonderful guy, but external control through and through. Can this work with only one of us using choice psychology?

It can, but not as well. Because your husband is so wonderful, I'm sure he'll try not to undermine any of the specific plans and agreements that you and your daughter work out. Still, he's a powerful presence in the family, and his continued reliance on external control will only become more visible as you become less controlling. The most important thing for you is to be honest and non-controlling with him. Let him know that you're trying something new, and that you'd love for him to join you. Just don't push. As your relationship with your daughter improves, he may like what he sees. Leave the book around; he may pick it up in his own time.

With choice psychology, we're finally getting somewhere with a disruptive, sometimes aggressive nine-year-old boy. We've stopped fighting with him, and we're trying to be more clear and consistent with our limits. I can see that things are gradually improving. The trouble is, our seven-year-old is crying "no fair." He thinks we've gone soft on the big guy and that his brother should be severely punished when he ruins everyone's evening. What do I tell him?

First of all, tell him that he's right. It isn't fair that his brother sometimes treats him badly. But also tell him that you're learning that the severe punishments don't really help you get what you want most. You want his brother to learn to be a better member of the family, and it is not something that you can force him to do.

Your younger son's desire to punish his brother is understandable. He, too, lives in this external control world that suggests that we use our power to force people to do what we think is right. What a wonderful lesson he's learning by watching you find a better way. Don't forget to show him how you're sticking to your limits and not giving in to his big brother's threats and control maneuvers.

The most surprising thing to me about choice parenting is that once I caught on, it was easier than what I was doing before. Can I use this same approach with other important relationships?

You not only <u>can</u> apply choice psychology to other relationships, I don't see how you can avoid it. Once you begin to see human behavior from an *internal control perspective, it just doesn't make a lot of sense to push and pressure and coerce. It's remarkable how quickly all of your relationships improve when you try hard to remove the control maneuvers from your daily behavior. I'm often asked if I believe that anyone can really change. My answer is this—we can't change who we are, but we can certainly change what we do. When we do that, we change our entire world.*

O.K, I'm ready to try something different from what I've been doing, which hasn't really been working all that well anyway. So how do I get started? Where's the best place to begin?

More than anything, choice parenting is a mindset. So where you begin is less important than how you begin. Start with something simple, perhaps a family resource that needs to be shared. Try talking with your child in a more connected way about the problem, and just focus on your own best attempt to stay connected. You might try to establish a new morning bathroom routine, or a new plan for sharing the computer. Don't begin with something that's very emotionally charged; you might have to wait a bit to take on homework or curfew issues. Start small, with the first couple of tools, and let yourself get the hang of talking about issues of conflict without controlling or being controlled. You'll know when it's time to take on the bigger issues.

As you gradually begin to think about your and your child's behavior from a choice psychology perspective, keep the following key concepts in mind:

- *Choose Connection over Control. When you're talking with your child about any issue, you always have two agendas. One is practical and control oriented—trying to solve a problem. The other is relational and belonging oriented—trying to stay connected with your child. Make the second more important than the first.*

- *Self-Evaluate. Be clear about what you're trying to accomplish, and evaluate how effectively you behave. Measure your success by how well you do, not by what your child does. "Did I keep my cool?"…"Did I use connecting language?"…"Did I try to learn about his perspective?" Better cooperation will come in time, as the connection strengthens and improves.*

- ***See His Best Attempt.*** *Try not to view behavior problems as transgressions or violations, but as your child's best attempt to meet basic needs. Instead of getting him to stop doing things, try to help him come up with better choices.*

- ***See the Sense in His Choice.*** *If you approach your child with the mindset that his behavior is ridiculous or outrageous, you have little chance of connecting. Remember, you want more than mere compliance—you're trying to raise a caring, responsible child. The best way to be influential is to stay connected, and the best way to stay connected is to see the sense in your child's (very annoying) behavior.*

- ***Choice Parenting Doesn't Mean Being a Wimp!*** *Commit yourself to stop fighting, not to stop setting limits. Don't underestimate your considerable power and influence. Be persistent. Tell your child what you want, and what you think is best. Stop telling him what he must do, **or else!** When he drags his feet or pretends he didn't hear, let him know clearly and calmly that you really meant it. When he falls short of his agreement, start the process over expressing confidence that he can do it.*

- ***Choose Not To Be Angry.*** *Remember the Total Behavior suitcase. Anger isn't something that happens to you, it's a response that you generate. If you continue to choose angry behavior, like criticism and coercion, you'll continue to feel angry. Try hard to choose more caring behavior, especially when things are not going your way.*

A FINAL WORD

Parenting your child may well be the most challenging job you ever take on. It can also be the most satisfying. For this to be true, I suggest you choose to be more of a gardener than a sculptor. Work hard to provide the best conditions for your child's growth, but understand that you can't determine the shape of his life. Remind yourself, especially when you and your child want different things, that staying connected is more important than overpowering. Learn to recognize the control imperative at work within all of us: When people aren't behaving the way we think they should, we're tempted to use our power to push them into line. Resist that impulse and you'll be a better parent. Find a way to keep the conversation going, to set your limits while protecting the cord that connects you. These are the tools that will help your child grow into a caring, responsible adult. These are the tools that will make you a choice parent.

BIBLIOGRAPHY
(* These titles recommended for parents)

Albano, A., Chorpita, B., and Barlow, D. (2003). Childhood Anxiety Disorders. In E. Mash, and R. Barkley (Ed.s). *Child Psychopathology.* New York: The Guilford Press, (pp 279-329).

Baumrind, D. (1991). The influence of parenting style on adolescent competence and substance use. *Journal of Early Adolescence,* 11(1), 56—95.

*Boffey, D.B. (1997). *Reinventing Yourself: A Control Theory Approach to Becoming the Person You Want To Be.* Chapel Hill: New View publications

*Buck, N.S. (2000). *Peaceful Parenting.* San Diego: Black Forest Press

Glasser, W. (1984). *Control Theory: A New Explanation of How We Control Our Lives.* New York: Harper & Row

*Glasser, W. (1998). *Choice Theory: A New Psychology of Personal Freedom.* New York: Harper Collins

*Glasser, W. (2002). *Unhappy Teenagers: A Way For Parents and Teachers to Reach Them.* New York: Harper Collins

Hinshaw, S., and Lee, S. (2003). Conduct and Oppositional Defiant Disorders. In E. Mash, and R. Barkley (Ed.s). *Child Psychopathology.* New York: The Guilford Press, (pp 144-198).

*Kaplan, L. (1984). *Adolescence, The Farewell to Childhood.* New York: Simon & Shuster

*Kohn, A. (1993). *Punished by Rewards: The Trouble with Gold Stars, Incentive Plans, A's, Praise, and Other Bribes.* New York: Houghton Mifflin

Lochman, J., White, K., and Wayland, K. (1991). Cognitive-Behavioral Assessment and Treatment with Aggressive Children. In P. Kendall (Ed.) *Child and Adolescent Therapy: Cognitive-Behavioral Procedures.* New York: The Guilford Press, (pp. 25-65).

Offer, D., Ostrov, E., and Howard, K. (1981). *The Adolescent, A Psychological Self-Portrait.* New York: Basic Books

Osman, B. (1997). *Learning Disabilities and ADHD.* New York: Wiley

Swartz, K. and Margolis, S. (2003). *Depression and Anxiety.* New York: Medletter Associates, Inc.

*Turecki, S. (2000). *The Difficult Child.* New York: Bantam Books

U.S. Public Health Service. (2001). *Report of the Surgeon General's conference on children's mental health.* Washington, DC: U.S. Department of Health and Human Services.

Wubbolding, R. E. (2000). *Reality Therapy for the 21st Century.* Philadelphia: Brunner-Routledge

Wubbolding, R. E. (1991). *Understanding Reality Therapy, A Metaphorical Approach.* New York: HarperCollins

0-595-32025-2

Printed in the United States
55407LVS00005B/70-72